MW00952813

Becoming Alive and Real

Journey into the Body's Truth

Cherie McCoy

Learn more about Self Acceptance Training at
http://www.selfacceptance.us/

In Memory of
Richard 'Dick' Olney

"THOUGH LOVERS BE LOST LOVE SHALL NOT;
AND DEATH SHALL HAVE NO DOMINION."

- DYLAN THOMAS
(From "And Death Shall Have No Dominion")

Thanks to:

Jason Miller, who gave me so many many hours of technical help creating my web site, teaching me how to create and send out my e-mails, doing it for me when I needed it, and formatting my book for publishing. And, of course, creating my book cover.

Morgaine Breimayer, for the Anahata symbol illustration (which represents the heart chakra) on the cover of this book.

Karen Adler who read and edited my book, spending hours on the phone going over it word by word with me.

My heartfelt gratitude to all of the people (whose names have been changed) who have allowed me to use their personal sessions as examples of this wonderful work, and all the students and trainees over forty-seven years who have learned the work and taken it into their lives and practices.

Also, so many thanks for all the people in my life, those who know and have experienced SAT and those who haven't, who have encouraged me to continue writing when I wanted to stop.

Table of Contents

Bibliography 122

Preface

As I reflect back on the last 47 years teaching Self Acceptance Training, I am still profoundly touched by how this work has enhanced and changed so many people's lives. With this book I am hoping to reconnect with many of you whom I haven't been in touch with, as well as those of you whom I have seen recently, to remind you of these incredible tools, and to encourage you to keep using them and to keep exploring that great frontier — that holy mystery called energy, your body. Every once in awhile I get a note from one of you saying you're still using the tools, even though you haven't seen me or been in a group for a long time. Nothing warms my heart more.

Those of you who are new to this work may find times when you feel confused, uncomfortable or even skeptical. I'm not trying to change any of your basic beliefs, and I hope that you will still find much of this helpful. Take what is good for *you* and leave the rest. Yet, if you are a seeker, searching for a sense of spirit, release from childhood pain, or unconscious reactions in adulthood, this book was written with the intention of helping you.

Now that my dear friend Don Schmauz (who also taught SAT) has passed and Dick Olney, who originated it, has been gone for many years, I have written about this wonderful work because so many people, over the years have asked both Dick and me if we would. Back in the day, Dick would say, "We are too busy doing it to write about it." So now I have put down some of it in words as best I can (because how can I describe what can only really be experienced).

I know that many of you who have been in professional trainings with Dick, Don, and me are now using SAT to some or greater extent in your own careers of therapy, teaching, nursing etc. Some of you have even taught the tools to your children.

This powerful work which has changed my life, my children's and grandchildren's lives and so many more will go on. And as Dick used to say, "Nothing is new". It's all been there for a long time and others are bringing forth more.

Walk in Loving Light,
Cherie

Attention: I have lost touch with so many of you over the years. If you have trained with Dick, Don, or me, are using SAT in your work, and wish to be included on my Community page at http://www.selfacceptance.us/, please notify me via the 'Contact' page.

Janie

She sat before me stone-faced, body uninhabited. She related all the details without any emotion, making it clear that she felt it was her fault because she had been drinking. They had invited her back to the 'after party' where she discovered that she was the only girl.   They raped her repeatedly, — brutally.   She reported that she went someplace deep in her mind and didn't resist —that was another reason 'it's her fault'. I told her she may have saved her life by being passive, that there was no way she could have fought off four of them. She was bruised, bitten and worst of all, robbed of her sense of self, her dignity, her self confidence and even her ability to feel.

She told me all the details, her beautiful brown eyes looking straight into mine, with a vacancy, her voice a monotone, as if she were reading from a very boring book. When she had finished, I asked her to close her eyes and feel her body.

"My body feels a little shaky", she reported.   "When it was all over, my body shook for a long time. It was really scary to shake like that."

"Yes," I replied, "And that was good!   It was the way your body released all that tension and some of the memory. It happens all the time in this work so if that is happening, just let it happen. And even though the shaking is scary, check to see if it is pleasurable or painful." She reported that it was scary and kind of pleasurable although she hadn't thought of it like that before.

I told her to keep her eyes closed, breathe and just feel whatever was there. After some silence, she reported feeling sad. She started to cry. "Good. This is a safe place to cry," I reminded her. She cried for some time. She then told me she hadn't felt anything since they started "having sex" with her. She had gone some place else and didn't feel any of it. The fact that she labeled it "having sex" rather than "raping" was another sign to me of how extensive the power of her denial and shame was.

Intuitively, I asked her, "Is this the first time you've cried?" The answer was, "Yes, except a little the day after, when I was alone." I knew she had told the story to nurses, friends, family and a couple of therapists. _No one_ had taken the time to let her feel her body and wait for the healing process.

Again, she told me she hadn't felt any of it. I explained that this often is the case in abuse situations. There is too much energy input at once and the person leaves their body. (The brain goes into what is called a 'brain freeze' by brain experts, and the experience is stored in the tissues of the body.) I refer you here to a presentation by Dr. Robert Scaer, _How the Brain Works in Trauma_ [1] on YouTube.

She repeatedly blamed herself because she had been drinking, stating that that was why she didn't press charges. She reported feeling guilty and ashamed and of course had no sense of her anger and rage. Instead she felt numb and depressed. After allowing her to cry for some time, I asked her to stand up, breathe, and bend her knees so the energy could come into her feet and she could really feel them. After a bit of time I handed her a towel and asked her to squeeze it and talk to these four men.

She started in a tiny, whimpering voice. I encouraged her to squeeze the towel and even to bite it. This engages the muscles in the throat, arms, back, neck and mouth, allowing the energy held there to begin moving and making it easier to verbalize the emotions held in the tissue. Soon her voice was full and loud and she was expressing her anger at them.

When she was finished, she reported that she felt so much better, "I feel strong. I have my self confidence back." Indeed, she had more color in her face and it was obvious to any onlooker that her tension, not only in her face but throughout her body had left. She was standing straighter and holding her body in a manner that reflected strength and confidence. In energetic terms, she was grounded [2] (feeling her body from the top of her head to her feet). I explained that she might have to do this a few more times, and to do it if she started to blame herself again.

This self-blame is typical of abuse victims, whether the abuse is from incest, rape, being beaten or even from verbal attack, (which is a beating of the aura or energy field surrounding the body). The humiliation of these shameful acts is embodied and the victim begins to abhor the body, and to lose their identity with it and instead identify with the action, *i.e. rape is bad, therefore I am bad.* When this happens, the person truly is lost since, as long as we are alive, we are this *body*, this *energy made flesh.*

What is Self Acceptance Training?

It is interesting that this is the last chapter I am writing and the hardest, because it has been difficult for me to define and explain this work. For years I avoided telling friends and acquaintances just what I did because Self Acceptance Training (SAT) is so experiential that when I would try, people would think it was too "woo-woo". Yes, it is "woo-woo" if you mean magical because at it's core, SAT brings us into our deepest potential. It lets our body talk instead of our head and it connects us to every other living being as well as to nature, and to the universe. It connects us to what primitive people knew and lived their lives by. Dr. David Perlmutter [3] tells us that science is now realizing that we can change our DNA and I believe connecting to our deepest self and learning from it is one way to do it.

Does everyone who does a session of SAT *know* this? No, but each time we touch into that unconscious place, we *know without knowing* in the Buddhist sense of the word, and one day, we find ourselves more open and knowing. And now that I have "woo-woo-ed" you out, I will try to explain in more layman terms. SAT is a teaching more than a therapy, although many therapists have trained with me and have incorporated it into their work. I am mostly teaching people to *trust* their body.

Because the body is pure energy, it contains our history and our life's truths which is a source of healing and knowing wisdom. By following its sensations and/or emotions, by allowing and staying with these sensations and/or emotions they will *change* and bring the person to their inner truth, their unconscious potential and to an inner level of self esteem that does not come from proving yourself in the world but from *knowing* your connection to it, to *knowing* that our deepest core is entwined with what the world calls "divinity" or "good".

This journey through sensations held in the body reveals truths that often differ from beliefs of the mind. I refer you to the chapter titled "I Can Deal With It".

Dick Olney, the originator of this work has said, "When you allow yourself to experience yourself exactly the way you are, without any judgement, analysis or effort to change, you will automatically change."

I would add that effort only creates collapse; judgement leads to distraction. When we stop judging ourselves, it is a lot easier to stop judging others.

"The highest form of human intelligence is to observe yourself without judgement."
- Jiddu Krishnamurti

Using many of the tools from Bioenergetics, Gestalt, Creative Fantasy, Ericksonian Hypnosis, Intuition, Energy reading, and grounding them in eastern philosophical traditions of Gurdjieff, Ouspensky, and Buddhism, I have found none is as important as the trust that the person develops in their body. I am always ready to throw out a tool and follow what is happening in the body.

This body journey will often lead to:

- Relief from anxiety
- Alleviation from guilt and self criticism

5

- Relaxation of body tensions / pain
- A sense of inner peace
- Greater spiritual consciousness

The knowledge of who we are within our own energy field (i.e. the body) is the greatest gift we have. If we don't work with the energy knowledge of the body, we cannot manifest our consciousness as it is meant to be. As far back as the mid 1930's Dr. Wilhelm Reich [12], contemporary of Freud, psychologist and scientist was telling us about energy held in the body, creating tensions and perhaps eventually, illness. Now other psychiatrists and neural scientists such as Dr. Robert Scaer [1] are echoing the same theory.

As I am working with a student, I view myself as an explorer, watching for what they are experiencing and giving a tool to help them deepen that experience. Then I wait to see if that tool makes a change. If it does, the person will go deeper into themselves and perhaps I will give them another tool to accentuate what they are experiencing. If it does not, I throw the tool out and wait for another tool to come to me from the person. This process takes an ability to sit in my own sensations, let go of any ego or need on my part to *help*, and trust that what *is happening* is what *should* be happening. This sitting within my own inner space allows the person I am working with to experience themselves in a similar manner. This is the hardest part for the facilitator-trainee to learn.

As you read through the sessions in this book, you will see that they are short. That is partly because once a student has learned to trust the body, things move faster than when you are coming from the mind and partly because a lot of the time is spent in silence while the participant is exploring their sensations or at the end when he/she is sinking into the truth and/or the peace of the body.

As the student continues to work with me over time, or if they come to a group where others are modeling the work and the tools, I encourage them to take these tools home and try the work in their everyday life. It is so edifying to me when someone calls me and tells me they have done a major piece of work all by themselves, or when I get a card or e-mail from someone I haven't seen in years telling me they are still using the tools as different situations come up in their lives.

I think it is amazing that the name for this work that Dick and I chose is Self Acceptance Training before we remembered that "SAT" in Sanskrit means God (or universe, or higher power or Spirit if you have trouble with the word God). "SAT" is that place of peace that comes to us in meditation, or (if you are like my father who did not think of himself as spiritual), you like to sit in a boat fishing for hours without saying a word.

We did not think of "SAT" when we were thinking of a name for this work but indeed, that place of peace is where most people end up after their experience and many meditators have mentioned that SAT is like a meditation into the body sensations with the intention of discovering something new about themselves.

So I can talk about Self Acceptance Training in so many different ways; energy flow, emotional and/or trauma release, specific tools to take you from a troublesome feeling to a sense of strength, a means of exploring trance states of meditation. No wonder I have had a hard time explaining it.

A woman was recently giving her story at a consciousness meeting. She revealed that she always wanted to be a more dynamic speaker and admired people who spoke with such excitement and were "charismatic". She spoke in a slight monotone and without emotion about her sad childhood of abandonment. When she revealed that she had taunted a young cousin about being fat, she began to sob and didn't stop until someone handed her a Kleenex. She then took a deep breath and resumed. Suddenly, she was speaking more fluently, with more authenticity, energy, and heart. She was even joking and exhibiting a relaxed demeanor. *She was charismatic.*

By allowing herself to be as sad as she felt, she changed and became more alive and flowing in the moment. This is Self Acceptance, (experiencing oneself without judgement, self-evaluation or self-observation). In other words, Self Acceptance happens when we experience without the mind or ego interfering. This was an example of how it can happen in our everyday lives, if we allow it.

We all want to be more attractive and our nation spends millions each year striving after that goal, not realizing that it is a person's energy that makes them attractive. It is their sense of aliveness, which sends forth charisma and attracts others to them.

Debbie, a fifty-eight year old student of SAT reported that she always attracts younger men who want to date her. They are attracted to her and tell her it doesn't matter how old she is. She has examined her innermost self for years, exploring her sensations, memories, and feelings about many of her life circumstances with awareness, allowing, and forgiveness. She is very in touch with her body, radiating light and aliveness.

As Dr. David Hawkins says in his book, Power vs. Force [11], *"Simple kindness to one's self and all that lives is the most powerful transformational force of all. It produces no backlash, has no downside, and never leads to loss or despair. It increases one's own true power without exacting any toll. But to reach maximum power, such kindness can permit no exceptions nor can it be practiced with the expectation of some selfish reward. And its effect is as far-reaching as it is subtle."*

You may notice that he mentions kindness to 'oneself' first. That is the hardest person to be kind to, and yet, when we are, when we truly forgive ourselves, when we stop judging, we come into this peaceful aliveness where our energy flows through our lives. Self Acceptance Training, first and foremost, teaches us to be kind to ourselves, leaving the rat wheel of the mind, and coming into the pleasure of who we are as a body, and even deeper, into our connection to the universe of energy.

Dick Olney

I met Dick Olney [5] in 1969, when he was first developing his work, in a Gestalt Training group that was meeting once a month. We later named this work Self Acceptance Training because we saw that at the moment of resolution, when the client allowed themselves to accept or experience 'what is', a great peace came over them and they felt more alive and real.

In the late 1960s and 1970s the Human Potential Movement was growing and centers were popping up all over the world. Esalen in California is the largest and most well known. As our relationship grew and we began living together, I learned that Dick had been instrumental in developing the Milwaukee growth center, Cambridge House. Because of this, he and I could attend any of the growth groups held there which were led by therapists coming in from around the country. Any time a really good therapist, especially those who were into energy psychology, came through we would be sure to be in that group, thus experiencing and learning many different views and styles of working with various modalities. These we took into our own work and tweaked them with our philosophy of *allowing* while watching and emphasizing '*what is*'. By this I mean that we waited for a sign from the student that something was changing and then gave them a tool to emphasize that change, thereby allowing them to experience it more fully.

When that happened, something else would change and then we would give them another tool etc. Dick's main interest was in hypnosis, and my own in meditation and the healing arts. We combined them with our own individuality so we each had our own style.

As a young man, Dick had become interested in Theosophy and studied with the Theosophical Society for some time. They recognized his genius and his photographic memory and wanted him to tour the country lecturing for them. He declined but later utilized that genius and his love of poetry, as well as his many other talents along with his charisma to develop and teach this wonderful work of Self Acceptance Training for more than twenty-five years.

Our spiritual interests were very eclectic and although we never aligned ourselves with a particular religion, we always saw the work as extremely spiritual.

A Buddhist teacher named Alan Watts [4] came through Cambridge House and he and Dick became friends. His teachings greatly influenced Dick and the Buddhist philosophy of *allowing* became the root of Self Acceptance Training. Thus Dick defined Self Acceptance as 'allowing myself to *experience* whatever I am, without criticism, self evaluation or effort to change'. He found that when a person truly immersed him/herself in this way in whatever they were *experiencing*, they would automatically change. Later in his life, he was very influenced by Native American teachings and then Shamanism.

Dick had trained with Fritz Perls, Alexander Lowen, John Pierocus, Virginia Satir, Charlotte Selver, Milton Erickson and many other great names in the Human Potential Movement. He had a lifelong interest in hypnosis and the English language and had taught English at the University of

11

Wisconsin. This, along with his photographic memory and his incredible ability to create poetry was a great combination for taking people into trance states. Since he knew that sound was one of the factors in taking people into trance, he often used chanting, drumming and, of course, his own beautiful deep voice.[5]

Because of this interest in trance states, he realized that when people were in one, they were more relaxed in their bodies and therefore more open to change and growth. Also, he realized the trance state happens naturally by just focusing on sensations and being quiet for a time.

This became one of the big differences in how we used the modalities of Gestalt, Bioenergetics, Creative Fantasy, and Sensory Awareness in what we were developing. The relaxed trance state along with the philosophy of *allowing,* rather than doing or fixing became a primary focus of Self Acceptance Training.

We were constantly checking in with the body. We found that the body would always respond to a spoken truth, even if the mind did not agree. This then became the thermometer of the work. So by checking for any slight or great change in the sensations, or by watching for a change in the breath or sometimes in small movements in the skin, the body's truth would be revealed.

Dick and I traveled the United States and Europe, teaching this wonderful work for many years. It changed people's lives including our own, as we practiced the tools with each other and on ourselves. One of the many blessings in my life is the influence his living and working with my children has been. I have also had the privilege of teaching some of these tools to my grandchildren. He used to say, "This work should be taught in homes, schools, and doctor's offices," and indeed, we have taught it to parents (as parenting tools), to teachers, doctors, therapists and even to artists and actors who report a change in the experience of their work.

In his later years Dick focused more on his love of hypnosis. However, he always worked from the clues of the body. He saw the body as a mirror of the great unconscious, just as dreams are, and where the potential of the individual resides. Remember, when I talk about the body I am not referring to what most people think of as the body. I am referring to this energy made flesh ----- this 'holy mystery' which all energy is.

As Roslyn Moore states in her book, Walking in Beauty, "Dick was an unthreatening, grandfatherly figure with a love of poetry, a wry sense of humor, mischievous eyes, and a very level head. He was personally acquainted with magic and was guided by almost unerring intuition. The great wisdom, inexhaustible endurance, and boundless patience he brought to his work will long be remembered." [6]

My Exploration into Light

We seldom think about our bodies being energy or our voices being energy or our thoughts being energy. And yet, everything IS energy. When I began to look at myself in these terms, my life became a great exploration and an exciting adventure. I began to discover that I was so much more than the personality traits which I had created to survive my traumatic childhood or in response to it.

Some of these I was proud of and others I judged harshly and hid from myself as much as I could. Of course other people saw these traits and unconsciously picked up on my judgments and judged them too. Using the tools of Self Acceptance Training, I began to face these character traits along with the accompanying emotions, behaviors and memories. By exploring my sensations along with my thoughts, I swam my way through my memories, emotions and old traumas to find that I was *PEACE*.

The more I explored myself without judging who I was, (or actually who I *thought* I was), the more I could let go of these judgments and sink into what I call essence. Essence is not something you can know at an intellectual level, it is only truly known experientially. It is that deep soft place of peace and calm where we feel somehow connected with the earth, the waters, plants, animals and our fellow humans. It is a place where the mind quiets down and we begin to know without knowing, in other words, experientially.

When we 'know without knowing', often concepts come to us later and we wonder, "where did I learn that". In fact we have connected with the Super Conscious where all knowledge resides. Our life begins to change; there is a balance within us that translates into our everyday living.

I became a different kind of person, more confident in my dealings with the world and with my family. I also found that, now that I wasn't judging myself so much, other people weren't judging me either, and when they did, I was somehow not as connected to it. This brought an absence of anxiety and the feeling of contentment to me. When I realized that other people's judgments are more about them than about me, I began creating love and peace in my life and in my relationships.

Here is an example of one of my own pieces of work in exploring who I am. I was being Rolfed [7] (a wholistic body technique in which the Rolfer releases tension in the facia of the tissue, often releasing memories and/or emotions and always changing posture so that the body falls more into alignment with gravity, resulting in an easier way of being/ moving in the body).

After one particular session, I noticed that I had a residual pain in the center of my chest. As I explored this pain with my guide/SAT teacher, breathing into the pain, I found my head turning to the right and my lips wanting to suck. Then I would be repulsed and angry. This happened over and over. Finally my teacher gave me a hand towel to bite. When I bit down on the towel, rage and tears flowed out of me and I had an experience of biting my mother's breast. This was very confusing as my mother and I had a very loving relationship.

15

Later, when I told her about this experience, she related that when I was born, it was during the depression and she was standing in food lines and not getting good nutrition. They thought I was a colicky baby because I cried all the time. Then the doctor discovered that her milk was not "good" and I was starving from malnutrition. I had no knowledge of this before that piece of self exploration but it was hidden in my tissue.

After that experience, I felt lighter in my chest, more open and more loving in my experience of life. Truly, I felt Light in my being.

Kabbalists tell us that when the "Big Bang" happened, not only did time begin, but an infinite force of positive energy which existed before the Big Bang, spread throughout the cosmos. This positive energy force is called Or in Aramaic, which means Light and exists in everything in varying amounts [20].

The great spiritual beings tell us we are primarily vessels of Light. When we clear out old behaviors, anxieties, obsessions, resentments, worries etc., that Light shines through. It is visible to others even though they could probably not put words to it. The more we empty ourselves of what we are not, the more room we have to expand into Light and the more time we have to do what we were born to do, basically to spread love, kindness and peace. So grow your Light vessel, and by just being you, you will change the consciousness of the world.

"That was the true light which lighteth every man that cometh into the world."
- *Bible*

16

"There are two ways of spreading light: To be the candle or the mirror that reflects it."
- Edith Wharton

"The pursuit of perfection, then, is the pursuit of sweetness and light."
- Matthew Arnold

"Light is still a light-even though a blind man cannot see it."
- Austrian Proverb

"Let your light shine within you so that it can shine on someone else. Let your light shine."
- Oprah Winfrey

"Our consciousness is like a vessel, a receiving entity that is also boundless. The larger this
vessel becomes, the more water we can draw from the well. The higher our level of consciousness, the more Light we receive. Our task is to open ourselves more and more to the Light by expanding the volume of our spiritual vessel."
- Michael Berg, Secrets of the Zohar

"---see enlightenment, dormant,
in everyone who comes before you.
You see the inmost Self and feel deep reverence.
Nothing is insignificant; everything has meaning,
Even in a blade of grass
You see supreme Light shining."
- Mata Amritanandamayi

Thoughts Can Be Runaway Horses

New Thought religions, are now telling us that thought creates our reality. Dr. Wayne Dyer [10], in his books and on his television series, tells us to keep our thoughts positive and focus on our intentions to create the world we want. Dr David Hawkins in his book, *Power vs. Force* [11], talks about energy fields which he calls 'attractors', some of which are negative, or weak, and others which are positive, or strong. He claims we are constantly drawing these energy fields into our lives with our thoughts.   Both of these men believe, as I do, that our attitudes and thoughts bring certain forms of energy toward us in the form of people, ideas, experiences, worldly goods, etc.

This is not new thinking. Kabbalists have been teaching this same doctrine for centuries. Recently the book and film, *The Secret*, has been teaching the same, that we are today what we have been thinking *believing*, and feeling in the past [22]. Also, New Thought religions, Unity and Science of Mind, teach that thought, held as belief, creates reality.

Certainly when we are feeling sad or angry, we can't just dismiss these feelings and feel happy and positive. We need to breathe, feel the sensations and express the feelings in some way, and then *let them go*. By experiencing the relief of these emotions, we have more energy to deal with the circumstances, or the confidence to trust that they will resolve themselves.   In this way, we can go back to an affirmative attitude which will bring more of these positive 'attractors' toward us.

For example, one SAT trainee has a child with an ongoing illness. At times the feelings of sadness and rage come up and she either goes off by herself to express them or comes to a group where she has a lot of energetic support and wails and rages loudly. She then returns to her life with joyful energy and thankfulness. If she were to try to hold these feelings in or to ignore them and try to stay positive, she would be stuck in depressed thoughts, low energy, and tension, maybe even ending up sick herself.

Self Acceptance Training emphasizes re-identifying with your body, its sensations and emotions. Once this re-identification happens the student has a 'safe harbor' to retreat to in times of stress, to feel instead of defending from ego and to express emotions in a healthy way. This allows us to engage the world with awareness of the history and in some cases trauma, that has been stored in our tissue. Over time this process of SAT leads to a sustained ability to spend more of our life in positive thought and a peaceful existence.

Rose came into my office with her head filled with fears. She was a wonderful spiritual teacher, running retreats in a certain spiritual modality. She was worrying that people did not like her, that other spiritual teachers didn't like her, and judging herself with fears that she may be a fraud. These thoughts were wearing her down.

I asked her to lie down, sink into the floor, and feel her body. I reminded her that she was not a spiritual teacher, she was not a wife, she was not a mother. These were all roles she was playing in her life. Indeed, she was truly, only a body of energy made flesh, truly a 'holy mystery' as no one really knows just what energy is.

In the spirit of SAT, allowing myself to be whatever I am and even exaggerate it, I then asked her to feel her body sensations and repeat the word worry, worry, worry, over and over and over. After some time, I asked her to say, how she was feeling and the answer was, "Peaceful". I then asked her to feel that peace and repeat the phrase, "I can only be whatever I am". She became very quiet after some time and I felt my own stillness. (I often ask people to repeat a phrase or sentence to explore what might happen in the body.) Soon she reported a floating feeling which was very pleasant.

Here is an example of how hanging on to thoughts and belief can take us into suffering.

Vera is in what she views as an impossible situation. She lives with a twenty something daughter who is non-functional and refuses to leave the house. This worries and distresses her immensely.

She came to the group with a terrific headache which would not let up. Knowing that headaches are usually anger, I worked with her for some time having her express her anger at her daughter. "It won't go away," she cried. "I'm just getting tighter and tighter!"

"Make yourself really tight," I replied. "Tighter. Tighter. Tighter." She did this until she couldn't anymore and then started to cry. She then tightened and stopped the tears. If she had allowed herself to sob, she would have felt some relief. However, she jumped back into her thoughts (stuck in her belief), exclaiming over and over, "It's never going to end, I'm stuck with her!" Meanwhile, the pain in her head was increasing. Again she said, "It's never gonna end."

I pointed out that this was a very deep belief that she was creating with negative thinking. I asked her to stand and reach her arms out in front of her, palms touching. I asked her to SLOWLY, SLOWLY open her hands to all the other options and resources in the universe, trusting that she did not have to know what these options and opportunities were right now, she just had to open to them. She took a long, long time opening, spreading her arms as wide as she could. Her body relaxed. Her face looked softer, younger. Her headache was gone.

A beautiful teacher, Reverend Ken Daigle who truly *lives* the principles of New Thought (a philosophy of positive thinking) has said, "Pain is inevitable, to be human is to feel pain at times, but we do not have to suffer. Suffering comes from holding on to old beliefs."

And this piece of work shows how we can get so caught up in our negative thoughts that they become beliefs that we are living by, creating a lot of stress. By coming into body sensations, by moving, we can come back to who we really are, not our thoughts or our beliefs, but a body that has the ability to think. I often talk about our thoughts being a team of wild horses. If we do not control them, they will run away with us, like a team of wild horses in the old movies.

Sound as Energy

Sound is another form of energy. Often people stifle their natural sounds as part of an unspoken taboo in our culture. I have witnessed parents so embarrassed about their child crying on an airplane (probably because their ears were in pain from the drop in air pressure as the plane descended), that they covered the child's mouth and nose to cut off their air. I've talked to people who have been told in hospitals not to make groaning noises even though the groaning made them feel better. And of course, many people take drugs at funerals for fear of crying, repressing their grieving process, when in more primitive cultures, people are allowed to wail and really express their loss.

Because sound sets up a vibration on the inner tube (biology tells us the body is a tube within a tube; the outer tube being the skin and the inner tube extending from the mouth to the anus) [2], any sound is healing to the organism. Children, before they are acculturated, naturally make all kinds of sounds. The adults at first think this is cute and sweet. At some point it becomes annoying or embarrassing and the child is told to stop. I sometimes have to work hard to teach my students how to overcome this learned taboo.

Studies have found that if you can get a very ill patient to just say the word "Thrust!" over and over, they will get better. Laurel Elizabeth Keyes, in her book *Toning*, says, "Frequently I have watched amazing results come about in illness by just causing the person to change his *tone* in speaking. Instead of a sucking-in tone, to *thrust* his words out with vigor. By using his own voice to do this, he seems to change the polarity of his 'field' and a healthy condition results.........The *th* sound is one of positive push. One could hardly draw in his last breath with a good '*th*' sound." [9]

She gives this account of working with a woman who thought she was dying and was too weak to speak on the telephone. "Give it more THRUST," I encouraged her, and finally, with some indignation, she responded, "I AM THRUSTING MY WORDS OUT." From that moment it seemed the force was reversed from negative to positive polarity. The next day she was not only out of bed, but was doing some housework, and on the third day she drove to a nearby town to hear a lecture. There was no return of the illness. That day of changing her voice pattern began the change of her health." [9]

We all know how good it makes you feel to sing—it heals. To express with sound any emotion, from joy to sadness or anger or fear, can be life changing. As children most of us have learned to tighten certain muscles in our bodies in order not to express emotions as sound. These muscles become chronically taut and stiff, resulting in chronic pain, sometimes changing our posture or in extreme cases, creating disease. That is why, in my work with people, I am always asking them to exaggerate their sound. "Louder, louder, more more," I always say. The louder the voice the more energy released, and the more energy gained.

At one time, I was riding in the car with my nine year old grandson. We had just been playing tennis for the last hour and he was very excited. He started whooping and was surprised and pleased when I joined him. His parents and brother are very open about sound but I don't think he expected

23

it from his grandmother. I have also enjoyed hours over the years speaking gibberish with my children and then my grandchildren. My children used to love to speak gibberish in a restaurant when the waitress would approach, thinking she would assume we were speaking a foreign language. Unfortunately they have all outgrown the delight I still have in speaking it.

Gibberish is a made up language of sound using the tongue, lips and muscles of the throat. You cannot *think* and do gibberish well. It is very spontaneous and experiential, releasing a lot of tensions in that area and potentially a lot of emotions. Often, when working with someone who is having trouble letting go of their thinking, I ask them to tell their story in gibberish, or I ask them to talk to that person in gibberish. They might have trouble making this transition, but if they are successful they move into their body sensations, where they can release emotions with strong sound.

Learning to Focus on Your Body Sensations

Many people, when I ask them what they are feeling, don't know how to answer me. I have to tell them I am looking for sensations or emotions. If they have no emotions, they often have a hard time distinguishing sensations. I have to ask them to look for tensions, looseness, tingling, movement, restricted movement, numbness, cold, heat, or just an awareness of some area of their body.

Some people only become aware of their body when they experience extreme pleasure or extreme pain. Most have to be taught that we are always in a state of varying degrees of pleasure or pain. These *slight* sensations of pleasure or pain are what make up the bulk of our lives. We have body sensations all the time and yet, we hardly ever pay attention to them. In our busy, intellectual culture, it is almost an unspoken taboo. And yet, at a very basic level, it is truly who we are as these sensations are manifestations of our energy flow. As I have so often stated, these body sensations are energy, *either energy moving* (pleasure) or *energy trying to move* (pain). Physicists tell us that everything is energy, so our bodies are truly energy made flesh. To know ourselves in this way, through our sensations, we experience our connection with the rest of nature and come to know experientially, who we really are.

We are not the money in our bank accounts. We are not the cars and homes we own. We are not the roles we play

25

(father, mother, teacher, therapist, CEO, etc.) and yet, we get so identified with all of these outer concepts that we lose track of the simple truth. We are energy made flesh. We know that everything is made of energy and yet, no one really knows what energy is.

This energy made flesh, which I call a Holy Mystery because no one really knows all of the components of energy yet, is always changing and yet remains the same, both on a massive scale as we age and begin to change shape, and on a daily or minute by minute time schedule as we interact with our environment.

We all can see this energy change in our outer physical body as we become older. We look into the mirror and wonder, "How can I look so much older and still feel the same?" The truth is that who we really are (some call this the soul, or you could call it energy), is never changing. I repeat, the soul, or energy is never changing. It's just here to learn lessons.

However we often neglect to see the subtle changes inside that are happening in each moment. Only when some strong emotion erupts or some physical pain comes up do we pay attention.

When I ask students what they are feeling, they often say, "Nothing." They are looking for an emotion and at that moment, there is none. They don't realize that we are always *feeling sensations* and what these sensations are and where they are, often tell me more about what is really going on than their conversation or story. As I guide them into their healing, I'm checking in on these subtle sensations of pleasure or discomfort. And remember, everything is pleasure or pain in the body. Where it is will often tell me whether it is anger, fear, joy or sorrow that is being manifested in tension (pain), or pleasure (movement).

It may be minutely painful or slightly pleasurable and I sometimes have to help my students to recognize this as we are always looking for something bigger. Yet, when we watch these slight sensations, when we actually spend some time with them and breathe into them, we find a wonderful path to self-growth.

I view these sensations as molecules of energy, either flowing or stagnant. Often, if the sensation is breathed into and observed, we can recover memories and/or emotions that have been stored in tissue, which the body is trying to release. Sometimes there will just be a sinking into peace. The body has it's own way of healing.

Dr. Wilhelm Reich (Reichian Therapy) [12] and Dr. Alexander Lowen (Bioenergetic Therapy) [2] have both claimed that our history is stored in the body. Often our body feels our history and our mind projects it onto present day life. There are two examples of this in the chapter, Lover Structure-Examples.

Dr. Robert Scaer [1], a psychologist and neurologist who has been studying the brain and trauma, talks about how trauma is carried in the tissue and needs to be released in his books, *The Body Bears the Burden: Trauma, Dissociation and Disease* and the *The Trauma Spectrum: Hidden Wounds and Human Resiliency*. He also explains it beautifully on the web in *How the Brain Works in Trauma* [1], a video about brain freeze and release. This video shows graphically how animals in the wild release trauma immediately while animals in cages, pets, or humans in the cage of culture store the trauma in their body.

The atoms of energy which are constantly flowing within this physical body can get concentrated, for instance in my head where it turns into a lot of thinking. This can be very productive if I am writing a book or if I have a job that requires a lot of thinking. It can also be detrimental if I cannot turn my thinking off and speak from the authenticity of my heart, or if I end up not able to sleep at night, worrying or obsessing about some situation.

If this energy becomes concentrated around my heart, I may give myself away, enabling others to take advantage of me, or becoming so bereft when I lose someone, I become unable to function. If this energy becomes stagnant around my knees, creating tension or pain, I may find myself in struggles with others or with myself. Likewise, if it is blocked in the shoulders and upper back or jaw I may be leaking a lot of anger, or I may feel a lot of anxiety if it is caught in the belly or diaphragm. Often the person will only experience the tightness of these places if they have learned to repress the emotions. The body is always revealing who I am.[2]

Working with a student over the phone who periodically has excruciating pain in her jaw and an inability to open it very much, I asked her if she had ever been sexually abused. "Not really," She replied, "except I had an uncle who used to stick his tongue down my throat when he kissed me goodbye." I asked her to feel the pain and talk to him. She became angry as she spoke to him so I asked her to go back to a time when he did this and do a Wipe Out fantasy while feeling her jaw. This is a fantasy in which she could become bigger than him and bite him or do whatever else she wanted, and then make sure he no longer existed on the earth. She was not to move but to feel her body as she did this. She came out of the fantasy feeling no pain in her jaw. I told her, "Sometimes the body screams at us with pain until we release it's truth." The next day she phoned me to tell me she realized this bout of pain in her jaw had come up after she had seen him recently at a family gathering. She realized now that she had been in denial about his actions.

Some children have, what some perceive to be, too much energy. So many people I have worked with have said, "Everybody has always told me I was too much." For a variety of reasons, some are just born that way, and some have been abused, learning to hold great amounts of energy within. Sometimes these people have trouble containing their energy. Some hold it in until they can't anymore and then explode, some get frenetic, and some make themselves sick. Some self-medicate with excesses of alcohol, drugs, sex or food in an effort to control this energy.

When you begin to view these experiences as energy, there are some very simple tools to change them. I'm offering some of these tools in the Tools chapter and you will see others demonstrated in the individual sessions.

About Emotions

Basically, there are only four emotions: fear, anger, sadness and joy. [8] Of course, we have many names for these such as resentment, rage, terror, anxiety, elation, bliss, loss, sorrow, overwhelm, etc. but we should always remember that they are all aspects of these four: fear, anger, sadness, and joy. Remember, everything is energy, and these emotions are again, energy that arises in the body when we give a value judgement attached to an outer circumstance. When the mind judges, "This is threatening and it will overwhelm me," I will feel *fear*. When the mind judges, "This is threatening and I can overcome it," I will feel **anger**. When the mind judges, "This is a loss," I will feel *sad*. When the mind judges, "This is fulfilling," I will feel *joy*.

Many enlightened beings have worked hard to let go of outer attachments and if they really have, they will be beyond these value judgements and not feel emotions. For the rest of us the challenge is to allow the feeling, to express it in a healthy way and relieve the charge of energy which has built up in the body. Sometimes this can take a number of explorations. Then (and often the hardest part) to keep our mind from going back to the circumstance. Letting it go, so we don't relive it over and over, rebuilding the charge in our body: this is where we find peace.

In our culture we have taboos against feeling emotions, and especially against expressing them. Because of this, we either hold them in, repressing them into tensions which can lead to chronic pain or even disease, or exploding them out in inappropriate and/or destructive behavior.

Dick used to tell the story of how a young boy was angry with his mother and smashed her favorite vase. The mother came in, discovered her vase in millions of pieces and punished the child. The boy got the message, "Anger is bad. Don't ever feel that again." He then repressed his anger where it caused tensions in the body, exploding out at times in rageful behavior. Often this type of repression is passed down, generation after generation.

Whether we acquired the taboo in that way or by watching our parents raging at each other in abusive situations, or by living in an environment where there was never a sign of emotion, most people have to learn what we all came into this world knowing, that we are emotional beings.

Although babies express emotions openly, small children learn from adults to express them in unhealthy ways. We either throw our emotions around indiscriminately and harmfully or we repress them and make ourselves tense and even sick.

I think it bears repeating that emotions get caught in the body, along with memories. We usually carry anger in our upper back and sometimes in the form of headaches. Fear is often held in the stomach, diaphragm, shoulders and calves, and fear of our anger is carried in our lower back. Joy and sadness are both experienced in the heart and lung area although they are felt very differently. With sadness or loss the sensation is often tenseness around the heart until it is expressed, whereas joy is experienced as an expansion and lightness.[2]

My stepfather suffered a tremendous loss as a young child when his mother left the family. He lived with his father in a boarding house where he was not allowed to express feelings and had to remain quiet at all times. He suffered from chronic Asthma. Breath is required in order to express emotions. When my mother passed, he again experienced a great loss and was not able to express it. A month later he developed congestive heart disease, where the lungs begin to fill with liquid. He was having a lot of trouble breathing. Knowing how hard it was for him to express and/or feel his emotions, when I would see his sadness come up, I would express to him how sad he must feel and how hard it must be for him to live without her. He would just nod and swallow. Soon he was feeling much better. Later, when he developed Alzheimer's disease, I would often express the feelings that I could see he was repressing, and I would always see him relax.

I have found when people are focused on a particular part of their body while expressing emotion, they often recover memories they had forgotten.

Once, while being Rolfed [7] on my back, I started to experience rage and fear. I started to say "I don't know what to do. I don't know what to do," over and over.

My Rolfer asked, "Where are you right now, Cherie?"

I suddenly realized I was eight years old, sitting with my father who was threatening suicide. I had done a lot of work on the anger I had stored in my back about that memory, but had not experienced the helpless feelings of that situation.

As babies we come into the world so in touch with who we are as bodies, so whole, so real that emotions are just a natural part of who we are and expressing them is energy that just flows through us. Some of us are lucky enough to have had parents who nurtured that part of us, but most have to relearn that natural flow of energy.

In relearning that flow, we also need to learn how to utilize these emotions without harming others. To shout or scream at someone, for example, is harmful to the energetic aura (the energy field which surrounds the body). How often have we felt kind of sick after a yelling match with a friend or partner? Think then, how a small child feels when yelled at. This is called emotional abuse because the energy of the sound (yelling or screaming), is hitting the child's aura or energy field. No wonder that child has to harden and tighten its tissues to protect itself, soon shutting down to all forms of expression and sometimes unable to allow affection in.

In Self Acceptance Training, I try to teach couples to have an agreement when they are NOT angry. They agree that when they are really mad, to either turn and yell at the wall if they need to yell, or to take a break, go into separate rooms and use some other techniques to release the charge of anger. The person who is being yelled at gets to point to the wall and say, "please." Yelling at the wall allows the other person to hear the content without having to defend against the energy assault. After the charge is released, either at the wall or in a different room, they will be able to come together and talk about the issue much easier. Parents are encouraged to take a timeout, release the anger away from the child and then return and talk to the child.

These behavior differences are not always easy habits to change but it is possible, especially if talked about before the incident occurs. A student reported to me that she had talked with her children about how she was going to go to her room when she got angry and work it out before she yelled at them.

The next time she started yelling, her daughter said, "Mom, remember........." and pointed to her mom's bedroom. Yes, even our children can help us to change old patterns.

The most important part of the work of Self Acceptance Training is to teach people to trust their bodies, and that their bodies are self-regulatory. In other words, that they can be safe to feel whatever they feel, even to feel an emotion as intensely as their bodies want, and they will always come to a place of peace at the end.

Spirituality

Just as everything is energy, or perhaps because everything is energy, so everything is also spiritual. Self Acceptance Training, by its very nature, is spiritual because it is about exploring the body, this energy made flesh with its sensations and emotions. The body's energy movement is very conducive to the spiritual experience and students often have profound altered state connections. A trainee who became a good friend confided one time after she had gone to live in a spiritual community, " I was so anti God before I met you, if I had known SAT was so spiritual, I would never have worked with you. Of course I'm still anti religious but now I know the *experience* of God." Yes, the true goal in this work is to experience our endless nature.

Below the outer experience of our daily lives, our outer circumstances, our problems and our accomplishments, below our emotions, tensions, and pleasures of the body, we come to an experience of pure energy flow. This is a peaceful state in which we feel an unspoken connection to the universe, to all of existence, a state in which we feel a bond with everything. A student recently called it experiencing, rather than knowing from an intellectual space, "the State of Grace". When students come to that place, I sit back in silence for as long as it lasts, knowing that they are now in the hands of the Inner Teacher, learning things that I could never teach them and perhaps things they will not consciously know for a long time.

I myself, having fallen into a state of meditation many times in my childhood, have experienced great changes throughout my life as a result. I did not know what these experiences were until I was twenty-five and began to have a meditation practice, which actually brought me to a knowledge of Gestalt before I really knew what *it* was. I was using it, counseling teens before I ever experienced it myself or knew that there was a therapy named Gestalt developed by Dr. Fritz Perls [13]. I believe I had connected with the Super Consciousness where all knowledge exists.

A long time student, who had a chronically ill child, admitted that he was afraid of death because he didn't believe in the afterlife. So great was this fear that he had at one time thought to take the family savings and pay for his body to be frozen so that when they developed a cure for whatever he died of, they could bring him back to life. Yes, there are actually people who do this. Obviously, this fear had also kept him from allowing himself to feel all of the emotions surrounding his chronically ill child.

During a workshop session, I asked him to close his eyes and go through his own death in a body fantasy (where you experience everything without outer consequences). We waited quite some time in silence and suddenly he said he had died and he reported it all being black. He was obviously in a deep trance state.

"There is this little bit of light though." I asked him to follow it. He then began to narrate this incredible after death experience (granted, he may have heard of these but he was now experiencing it) in which he followed the white light through a long tunnel that ended in a beautiful garden. He then found himself way out, billions of miles into the universe. "Wow! Wow! I'm expanding into Love. I'm so full of love!"

He went on like this until he was again silent. The whole room was filled with light. People were silent for a long time and later reported feeling in an altered state along with him.

After this experience, each time he came to work with me, he was able to explore his sensations and emotions in a way he hadn't before.

I learned that a woman who had been studying with me off and on for thirty years had contracted a rare form of cancer. When I called her at the hospital she dismissed the person who was sitting with her by saying, "This is my spiritual teacher; I need to take this call". I was a bit surprised. I have been called teacher, healer, and even therapist but never knowingly called 'spiritual teacher'. This only underlined for me however that this work is so very spiritual. She went on to tell me how scared she was, that she did not want to die. I asked if she was feeling the fear in her body and she said "Yes." I then asked her to focus on those sensations and say, "I'm terrified! I'm terrified!" After doing this several times, she began to cry. I encouraged her to let the tears flow and after some time I asked her to repeat, "I'm terrified," and to add, "and I let go and I let God." After saying this a few times she became very silent for some time and finally said, "I feel peaceful now."

By first acknowledging the fear, and expressing it, giving vent to the tears of loss and fear, she was then able to give herself over to the peace and trust that 'all will be well'.

I told her she may have to do this several times a day and also to use other tools I had taught her such as wailing and moaning. She would have to do this into a pillow as long as she was in the hospital since they probably wouldn't understand that she was taking care of and bringing much relief to herself.

Although it is imperative to feel the emotions that come up, the most important task when dealing with a circumstance so frightening is to rein in the mind, not to let yourself dwell on or wallow in certain thought patterns. Rather, if you can focus on a sensation and repeat just a couple of words over and over and over until something changes, you will release the fear because you have felt and expressed it. To dwell on negative thoughts is to invite your most catastrophic fear. This truly is Hell. To alleviate this Hell you must be ever mindful that you are NOT your thoughts and stop them before they carry you away. There are many tools to accomplish this, but basically you can use anything to take your mind off the fear.

The important part of course, is bringing your attention to the body sensations as you do this. I always remind people that we do not always have emotions but we always have sensations which we experience as pain or pleasure. If I focus and breathe into either of these long enough, they change to something else, often ending in peace. Fear is the opposite of Love and by focusing on my body sensations, I am validating as well as loving myself.

Remember, you always have a choice—to focus on the thoughts or to focus on the body sensations. If you continue to focus on the sensations, you may or may not come into emotions, but eventually there will be an end to the thoughts and peace will come because that is the natural condition of the body. It is who we truly are. If you have ever had a 'good cry' where you allowed yourself to sob and maybe even make sounds, you know what I'm talking about. The body slows down and you feel peaceful.

A later note: this student has worked diligently with herself and has remained cancer free for ten years.

Peace, of course, is the main spiritual experience and if we stay focused on the body long enough we may come into an experience of expansion which is extremely pleasant. Some people have other spiritual experiences which they call mystical and some search their entire lives to have just one. These are great but as one of my spiritual teachers once told me, "These are just teasings to make you want to explore the expansion of peace more. The real goal is to *LIVE* in peace." Thích Nhất Hạnh, the great Korean Buddhist teacher, also teaches this. I have known people who have meditated one to two hours and had incredible experiences in meditation, then lived the rest of their day in anger and misery. This is a sign that they have energy blocks in their bodies (memories and traumas) that they need to release.

In 2011, I had the honor of spending an afternoon with Barbara Marx Hubbard, the author of Birth 2012. This amazing octogenarian had a mystical vision in 1988 where she experienced how the planet could be changed with the emergence of a lot of light at the end of 2012, when the Mayan calendar said it was the end of time. She had been working throughout the world to create what she calls hubs of change. Our large group was a hub of people, which she gathered into small groups who wanted change in Media, Health, Education, Business, Politics, Spirituality and more. In our small groups of 3-6 we sat with our hands over our hearts in meditation for a while, then just looked at each other in silence for a bit before we shared what we were doing in our lives to model love in our sphere of interest.

The goal, we know is not attained by proselytizing but rather by actual works of the heart. So we talked about how each of us saw more 'behavior from the heart' developing on the planet.

In my small group, people shared experiences of listening to friends' tearful stories of loss, volunteering for hospice, teaching people to meditate etc.

I shared about how Dr. David Hawkins [11] views meditation as a way of helping the world's troubles. He looks at each of these problems as a ship that is stuck on a sandbar. By meditating, we raise the spiritual consciousness of others (there have actually been studies that confirm this) and it's like raising the waters, so the ships can again float free. There are actually studies that have been done showing that certain neighborhoods who have people who regularly meditate, have less crime [21]. That is why I teach meditation in my work and encourage people to have a daily practice.

The Universe, Yahweh, Higher Power, Divinity Within or whatever you want to call that Ocean of Love that most people call God, dwells in all things as well as in our bodies and in our hearts. However, we are humans, having suffered human trauma and loss in our lives, and each of these are held in our tissue as energy blocks. Because we have bottled the trauma in the tissue, we have also developed certain behaviors in order to survive in that original set of circumstances and in similar situations.

These behaviors were our friends (they were rafts that saved us on that terrible river of childhood) and then they went underground where they continue to be used unconsciously, often creating troubles in our lives. They, along with the chronic tensions (energy blocks, i.e. traumas) in our bodies, keep us from living fully 'in love', in our lives. When we live fully 'in love', we live a truly spiritual life and it radiates outward in all that we do. This is the goal of our inner essence, our soul. I believe our life is our greatest spiritual practice. And just like a practice of meditation or Tai Chi or physical workout, it has ups and downs and many lessons to learn. It is important in any practice not to judge ourselves and to learn the lesson.

I use a lot of different guided image meditations in my work and I will relate one of them that came out of a piece of work a young person was doing. I really believe that everything in the universe is so connected that events around us are always underlining what is happening to us and teaching us, if we take the time to be aware of them. This is an example of that.

The workshop was in a home, high in the hills above Berkeley, CA. She was crying because she had such negative feelings towards her mother and really wanted to change them but, as she said, her mother had never been tender with her, had never nurtured her. As she continued to cry, someone in the group pointed to the patio right outside of the sliding glass door in the far corner of the room where a mother deer and her fawn had come out of the woods, had laid down on the patio, and were licking each other. Utilizing that synchronistic phenomenon, I asked her to pretend that she was that fawn and her mother was the mother deer. I asked her to keep her eyes closed and feel her body as she experienced this. She became very quiet for a long time and it was evident that she was very deep inside herself.

She had connected with an unconscious memory that, at some point, her mother *had* been nurturing to her. Babies who are not nurtured by someone often die. Her acceptance of the nurturing memories brought her to a spiritual connection in that deep quiet at the end of this meditative body fantasy. When she opened her eyes and came back to the room, she looked very young and rosy cheeked, the way babies look after nursing.

Your History Is In Your Tissue

"I don't know what I want to work on," she said as she laid on the floor with her eyes closed, breathing. "That's okay," I replied. Your body knows. Breathe some more and take a journey through your body. Then tell me what sensations you're aware of."

After some time, she announced that her jaw was tight and so were her knees; Particularly her left knee. Knowing that resentment is held in a tight jaw, struggle in the knees and that the left side of the body represents males in your life [16], I asked her what male she was feeling resentful at. She replied, "Rob comes to mind but now he has finally committed to me, it can't be him." I asked her to focus on her knees and say, "Rob, I'm still struggling with you." She said this a few times and her knees started to feel better. Then she said, "I want".

"Keep saying that and let your mind play with it," I replied. Soon her body was jerking, a sign that deep tensions and memories are being released.

"I want to say, I want more food — but that doesn't make sense."

I encouraged her to stay with it. "That's okay, trust what comes," I said.

"I want more food, I want more food, I want more love", she went on for a bit. Suddenly she was sobbing, "I want to be held." Her voice was tiny. Knowing she had been in an orphanage, I asked her how old she felt. "I don't know."

"That baby in the orphanage didn't get enough holding," I said. She continued to sob for some time. I waited for the transition — when the body has released the trauma and takes deep breaths. The calmness shows throughout.

When this happened I asked if she felt the change. "Yes — that is the first time I felt preverbal. Wow. It *is* all stored in the tissue."

This is an example of how early, even preverbal traumas get stored in the tissue and then tagged to later relationships.

I'm always telling people that Dr. Wilhelm Reich and Dr. Alexander Lowen came to believe that each person carries their history in their body tissue". Recently, neural scientist, Dr. Robert Scaer [1] has proven this theory with his video, *How the Brain Works in Trauma*, on YouTube.

Ian came into my office complaining of extreme anxiety which had plagued him for many years. He said he had been bullied throughout his school years, and then beaten up by five males several years ago when he was walking through a park with a friend. One of them had made a remark about his pretty face and accused him of being gay.

Feeling threatened, he and his friend turned to leave the park. They were accosted, severely beaten and had to be taken to a hospital. Worst of all, this anxiety was with him every day since. Anxiety is always fear. In this case, with his history of being bullied, he had probably learned to repress the anger, feeling safer with the undefined fear.

As he went into his body sensations it was evident that he was holding a lot of anger. As he talked to the young men, his back and shoulders began to tighten and hurt. This represents to me that there is a lot of energy held there and is

44

starting to let go, as pain is energy trying to move. I asked him to do a *Wipe Out Fantasy* in which you have extreme strength and abilities. You do not move anything in your body, but you *feel* your body as if you *are doing* everything.

This technique is often used by athletes before they perform to physically rehearse the moves that they will be making.

Fantasy is a watered down experience in which you can feel the action and act out things without any real consequences and without any real intention to harm the person. In this particular fantasy, you get to experience your rage at a person, releasing it in a safe environment and the person doesn't know it, so there is no repercussion and the result is that you feel more relaxed. You can do outrageous things like mow them over with a tractor or stuff them into a garbage disposal etc. At the end of the fantasy you *must* do something to remove them from the face of the earth so they no longer exist such as stomping them into the ground or throwing them into space. This is important for closure and imperative to complete the fantasy so that the body lets go. Therefore the name, *Wipe Out Fantasy*. If the student comes out of the fantasy and does not feel peaceful and pleasurable, I know they haven't wiped the person off the face of the earth. I then ask them, if they are willing, to go back into the fantasy and finish it.

Ian at first, objected, saying he did not believe in violence. When I explained that this was not doing anything violent to these men, that was not his intention, but was just a way to discharge his anger (which was repressed and being experienced as tension and anxiety), he agreed to try it. I reminded him that for relief to happen, he must end the fantasy

45

with them wiped off the face of the earth so they no longer exist.

He was quiet with eyes closed for some time and I waited for him to respond. When he opened his eyes, he reported feeling much better and the anxiety was gone. "I feel peaceful," he said. When asked how he finished he replied, "I threw them out into the universe."

Over a period of time, Ian was able to work out other traumas which he carried in his tissue and spend most of his time feeling comfortable in his body. Dick used to say that to feel comfortable and/or peaceful even 80% of the time in our stress filled society is a miracle. Many people aren't even aware that they are carrying stress and tension, or even pain.

Tools

These are just a few of the many tools I use in my work . You will find more in each chapter of this book and there are more that I haven't mentioned. Many have come from different modalities that I use and many have come to me as I have learned to trust my intuition and creativity. There are more out there because nothing is new. All knowledge already exists and is waiting for us to open to it.

Meditation

The state of meditation is one of the main goals of SAT, I always open a workshop with it and hope people will take this tool into their daily lives. Often the student will come to this place naturally, after exploring some troubling aspect of their life or having an emotional release. When this happens a deep sense of peace comes over the whole room, affecting everyone. We are all affected by each other's mental states. When we sit with an accomplished meditator, it is much easier for us to sink into a deeper meditative state. A similar experience happens when we are around people who are agitated. We can pick up their agitation. Although we all have this ability, some are more sensitive. They are called *empaths*.

Once, while working with a student in my home, my little dog Bodhi, who usually lies very quietly next to me, was rather restless. I had to keep petting him to keep him still. Suddenly, the person I was working with who had been talking extensively, went into a deep trance and Bodhi put his head on my leg and totally relaxed for the rest of the session. He had gone into trance also. I always encourage this state by suggesting the person let their body sink, telling them they are now in touch with the 'inner teacher', learning truths that are not apparent now but will be when they need to know them. I then sit with them in the silence until they come out of this wonderful state. The goal in meditation is to quiet the mind and dwell in a state of peace where there is little or no thought and everything seems slowed down.

One of the quickest paths to the meditative state is to focus on the breath, follow your exhalation all the way to the end and pause for a few moments before you inhale [14]. After a few breaths like this, your natural breath will resume and you will go quickly into a calm and peaceful place because the exhalation and pause before inhaling moves the energy out of the head toward the feet, relaxing the diaphragm as well as the rest of the body. I call this technique 'the secret of the sages' because it really enhances meditation. The more you practice this breathing, the deeper you will go into trance. Breathing this way is also a means to keep you focused or to bring you back to focus. It is also important to treat the mind gently, bringing the thought process back, again and again to the breath.

This Meditative Breath is also a powerful tool to use when you have fear or anxiety. By focusing on the breath throughout the exhalation and then pausing, the diaphragm relaxes, releasing fear, and energy flows downward. The person then feels like they can cope with the situation. I use this technique when I'm in an airplane with a lot of turbulence. It is a wonderful cure for fear of flying. Wiggling your toes also helps because this too brings the focus and the energy down to the feet, creating a grounded feeling even thousands of feet above the earth.

This type of breathing also works wonders for women in labor. The body relaxes, the mother can slip into a meditative trance and the baby doesn't have to work against tight tissue (i.e. tension and fear). Women I have taught to breathe this way report shorter labors and often experience little or no pain. Dr. Grantly Dick-Read talks about this breathing in his book, *Childbirth Without Fear* [14].

Contemplation

Contemplation is different from meditation in that the mind is used to think about something while you quiet the body by being still and breathing. Often insights will come in this state. The important trick is to focus on the body and not get carried away with your thinking. The SAT student starts every session with this, by focusing on the body and allowing the mind to bring up whatever is important. Sometimes the student actually has an agenda they wish to explore by thinking about it while watching the body. When a particular sensation stands out with a particular thought, the student breathes into that sensation and explores the thought, words or images that come. By remaining with the sensations, many different experiences may happen, bringing the person to their own individual bodily truth.

Jumping Rope & Temper Tantrums

People often ask me how to work with depression. Depression is a state of low self-esteem, low energy and low movement. It often, if not always is repressed anger. Two of the best tools for this are jumping rope or a temper tantrum. The movement of the arms, back and legs in both of these exercises generates a charge of energy in the body.

I often have the person say all the things they hate in their life while jumping. One woman I worked with had been hospitalized every spring for several years with depression. She was a teacher who hated her job, was chronically behind in her work and of course, by spring she felt totally burned out. While working with me, she jumped every morning while yelling all the things she hated about teaching school. She never was hospitalized again and she actually started to like her job more. You will find more about her in the chapter on the Perky Grandma.

The temper tantrum is one of the exercises developed by Dr. Alexander Lowen [2] in his use of Bioenergetics to take a person back to child like ways of expressing anger. Most parents have a hard time watching and/or allowing their child to have a tantrum because of fear that the child is out of control. They do not realize that the body is a self regulating system. This fear is passed down generation after generation when the parent stops this natural expression and the child gets the message, 'my anger is bad, don't feel it' or 'my anger is scary, it might never stop'. When my granddaughter went through a phase of temper tantrums we would allow her to flail with her anger and just like a good cry, she would come to a place of peace. My daughter would then pick her up, cuddle her and validate her feelings by saying, "You're having a hard time right now, huh." The little one would whimper, snuggle into my daughter's neck and nod her head.

John is an SAT student who has trained with me for several years. He reported being so depressed one summer that he actually couldn't get out of bed. He found himself with many negative thoughts and then decided to check into his body and actually found that he was enjoying lying in bed and doing nothing. Realizing that he didn't WANT to get up and do all the things he had to do, he decided to do a little SAT work with himself. He began with a temper tantrum. As he lay in bed he started kicking his legs and slapping his arms and hands on the mattress. He started saying all the things he didn't want to do. "I don't want to get up. I don't want to look for a job. I don't want to send resumes out to people. I don't want to do the laundry. I don't want to make phone calls, etc." Soon he felt much better, got up and did all the things he had to do and has not been back to bed in the daytime since. This kicking either with legs straight or bent and beating with flat hands, can physically express and release a lot of repressed anger and alleviate depression. Often, by just speaking our truth, even if it seems negative, something is released so that we can swing to the opposite experience or emotion.

Stomping

Stomping your feet is a wonderful way to bring the energy down to your feet and feel more grounded. I use this technique with people who are having a hard time taking their stand in their life, or if someone is scared. I have even used it with a teen that was having a bad reaction to a drug he was using. Once the energy is in your feet, (your feet are actually energetically connected to the earth, the largest amount of energy in our near vicinity), the same circumstances which were overwhelming or terrifying seem easier to deal with. You feel like you can cope.

Dianne came into my office crying and reported that she hadn't been able to really stop since her partner had left her three days ago. She was worn out and looked it. I had her stamp, making sure she came down heavily from her hip with each foot. Many people will march, with the thrust of the movement going up instead of down, which will keep the energy up. When I see this happening, I ask the person to pretend they are putting their hip through the floor. The point here was that I wanted to bring her energy down out of her heart and into her feet. After stomping and toning, using a long Ohhhh sound all the way to the end of the breath for awhile. she felt much better, had some color in her cheeks and looked softer. She reported feeling stronger and more secure than she had in the last few days.

I also use this tool when people get *stuck* in their feelings, going on and on in some emotional expression. Basically when this happens it is because the person is caught in some thought, their energy is all up in their head, and they won't let themselves really *feel* their body. An example of this was a young girl who would be sent to her room when she was angry and was allowed to scream, rant and rage for one half hour at a time, which she did, often wreaking havoc on physical parts of the room. If someone is really feeling their feelings, the emotion doesn't last very long. It changes. When it lasts too long, they are caught in their thinking and sometimes dissociated from their body. I stop them and gently bring them back to body sensations where they can feel and complete their work.

Wringing a Towel

Releasing anger is something that is very hard in our culture. We are either taught to repress it or taught through modeling, to express it in unhealthy ways. Many of us have been taught as children that our anger is bad, either from an experience where we had expressed anger and been chastised for it, or from witnessing rage and abuse between parents.

I teach people to find a place where they are alone and won't be disturbed, then to wring a towel and/or stomp their feet while pretending to talk or to yell at the person they are angry at, even biting into the towel, screaming at the person (turning a TV up loud if they are afraid of being heard). This releases their charge of energy around the situation and at the person.

Often they can then go back into the situation and either let it go, or talk to that person from a more rational place. Wringing a towel, as described in the Janie chapter, can assist the expression of anger by releasing the tension in the back, arms, throat, and mouth. It's important to stand with knees bent and breathe while focusing your eyes on the small space between your hands and thinking about the person you want to talk to for about a minute before you begin. This allows the charge to build (breathing) and also allows the energy (voice) to be directed at the towel.

The I-Thou

Often people leak a lot of energy by telling stories *ABOUT* someone. This does not discharge the energy they have stored around that person or situation although they may feel some relief. In other words they will still be very angry and find themselves telling the "story" over and over. Also the person listening may pick up the anger and feel upset him/ herself, or at least, find it hard to listen. I ask people to pretend that person is there and speak *TO* them, or to pretend that situation is a person and speak *TO* the situation using the word 'You'. This will bring up the full charge of energy that the student is holding and discharge it, allowing the body to come to a resting place. Again, once the charge (held energy) is discharged, the person will find it much easier to deal with the person or situation. Check out the chapter, Finding The I-Thou Experience.

Often I have to teach a spouse to use this Gestalt tool of talking **to** the person they are angry at, facing away from their partner, rather than telling their partner **about** the situation. Talking **about** the situation will often result in the partner taking on the **charge** of angry energy the spouse is carrying. (One student actually got so angry listening to his wife's **story** of what happened at work that he called the boss and got entangled in the affair). I never let a student tell me **about** or **the story of** their anger. This is how many therapists get burned out, listening to angry client's angry stories (particularly if they are an empath).

Stepping Into Someone Else's Shoes

This technique requires letting go of your own view, prejudices and even insights and trusting that somewhere in you lies the other person's truth (after all, we are all connected energetically). Often when I ask the student to step into the other's shoes, *they* are still talking. Here is an example.

Elaine was presenting that she had been in an unhappy marriage for many years and needed desperately to get out as it was affecting her health. However she could not bring herself to leave because of what happened in her family of origin. It was obvious that there was a big emotional block around this and I asked her to say more about it. When she revealed that she came from a broken home and had promised herself she would never do that to her children, I had her pretend her mother was there and talk to her.

"You ruined our lives!" she yelled. "How could you do that to us!! You were so selfish!! You only thought of yourself and because of YOU, I have stayed in this marriage all these years and been so unhappy. I refused to do that to my children and now that they are in their twenties, I still can't do it to them. It's all your fault! I will never do that to my children, even though my health is bad. I feel like I'm dying. I just can't hurt them the way you hurt us." She was crying bitterly.

I asked her to be her 'young' mother and talk to Elaine. As she began, it was obvious that *she* was still talking. "I didn't care about anyone but myself."

"Wait," I said. Then I asked her to step to a different place, close her eyes and let go of Elaine. I asked her to really let herself *feel* her 'young' mother, to take lots of time to slip into her 'young' mother's shoes. She was silent for a couple of minutes. Then she spoke. "Elaine, I'm *so* sorry I hurt you. I never meant to hurt you or the other children. I was so lonely in that relationship, I felt so unloved that I couldn't give you kids any love. I had nothing to give to myself or to any of you. Then this man came along and loved me. I could love myself and you kids again. But I am *so* sorry that it hurt you."

She opened her eyes, stepped back to her original space and said, "I can do it." She went on to explain that now, after all these years, she understood that her mother must have felt the same way she had been feeling in her marriage.

Biting A Towel

There are a number of people who have come to me complaining that their work environment is so hostile, they end up filled with rage, and have a hard time focusing on what they should be doing on the job. I advise them to carry a thick washcloth to work with them. When they begin to feel angry they are to go to the restroom, stand with their knees bent and breathe so the energy can move toward their feet, stuff the washcloth into their mouths, bite and growl or make angry sounds or at least *pretend* they are screaming at the person all the way to the end of the breath. Again, this allows them to release the charge and they report being able to go back into the work environment with more clarity and calmness.

Sound

Sound is another tool that can be used to release a charge of energy or to generate energy. In Bioenergetics we talk about the body being a tube within a tube, the inner tube being the tissue from the mouth to the anus, and the outer tube being the skin. Making sound creates a vibration on the inner tube, which radiates through the tissue toward the outer tube, causing relaxation and an increase of energy. It seems to create whatever the body needs at the time. At times I have the student make the sound, "Ahhhhh..." or "Ohhhhh," all the way to the end of the breath over and over for a period of time (Toning). Often this can lead to emotions such as crying or yelling or even laughter. The body's own truth emerges.

Another way we use sound is in yelling into a towel (if there is a sound problem), or just yelling. Although I never condone yelling at a person and it certainly is inappropriate to yell in public, if you are alone or with someone you trust, yelling can be a wonderful tool to release a charge of energy. If you live near a body of water, this is a great place to yell, or in the car. As I have stated in another chapter, I ask couples to make a pact. This pact allows the one who is being yelled at to request that the other yell at them facing the wall. This allows the other to hear the issue without taking the brunt of energetic sound against their aura, the energetic field which surrounds the physical body. Of course, this pact should be made before the couple are having a dispute.

Many couples have shut down their hearts because of this 'breaking the aura' that happens when they yell at each other. When angry sound hits the aura we tighten and actually create an armoring in the tissue, particularly in the chest and heart areas. Then we have a hard time feeling the love that is directed towards us, or our love for the other person. This happens a lot with children who have been yelled at a lot (emotional abuse). They tighten their body to defend against the energy hitting them and eventually they are shut down and don't feel any emotions, often until they are adults. They often then continue the pattern of abuse against their own children.

Mantra

Mantra is a wonderful tool in quieting the mind and we all need to work with this to alleviate the time and energy we spend in worry, fear, anxiety and useless thought. The Hindus refer to the mind as an elephant, walking through the bazaar. He grabs at everything until they place a stick in his trunk. Then he is peaceful and walks quietly through the marketplace, in control. The mantra is like that stick. Whatever mantra you use, whether it is the Sanskrit "Ohm" or the English word "One" or the name of your favorite deity or a short sentence like "All is well", the idea is to focus on the word or words and say them very slowly. I often tell students to say the mantra as if it were a blade of grass, growing very slowly.

A mantra can be anything and many people use affirmations for their mantra such as, "I am healthy in mind spirit and body." Here are a few of my favorites. "I give thanks, for help unknown, already on the way," (originator unknown). "All is well. All is well and all manner of thing will be well," (from St. Julian of Norwich). "Ohm Amriteshwaryai Namaha" (Sanskrit meaning I bow to the Sweet Goddess who dwells within).

Cate came to me complaining that she was very upset with her son who was dating a woman she did not approve of, even though she didn't know why. In exploring, she discovered that she really was trying to control the situation and that was a habit of hers. I gave her the mantra, "I Let go and I let Cate." She laughed and said, "Yes, I should really say, "I Let go and I let God." I corrected her, telling her, "I Let go and I let Cate," was much better for her because it would remind her of her control issues and would allow her to laugh at them instead of judging them. That is how SAT heals the judgment. In changing any behavior, we must first be aware of it, then catch ourselves and instead of judging, practice or even exaggerate it in a way to make it a caricature or funny. Eventually, after this practicing with awareness, the behavior will just let go.

Re-Taping

This is a wonderful tool to help the person who is emotionally *stuck* in a traumatic experience. Very much like EMDR [18], it takes the experience from one side of the brain where it is being relived over and over, across the corpus callosum (the nerve fibers which connect the hemispheres of the brain) to the other side. This allows a more integrated emotional feeling in the participant. When Dick and I were vacationing in Mexico one winter, he was asked to speak about and demonstrate the work. The woman who volunteered to work with him, had been in a very scary airplane experience where the plane had dropped at an incredible speed for a period of time. She had never really recovered from the experience and had recurring headaches. Dick asked her to go back in her body sensations to that time, only *this* time she would remain calm, trusting that all would be well, that the pilot would regain control and she would soon be safe at home. She was quiet for a long time and finally opened her eyes and said, "I went through the whole fall without the headache." At the end of the week, she told us she had been headache free all week.

This demonstrates the power of the mind to heal.

Introspection and Awareness

Introspection and awareness are two of the most important tools a person needs for change in their life. Without introspection you will never know what has influenced and is influencing your life and without awareness you have no chance for change. Change begins with awareness and in order to be aware you must be introspective. Not that I condone telling *your story* over and over and wallowing in the hardships of the past, but if I never look at how the past has and is influencing my present attitudes, beliefs and behaviors I am truly stuck in unconscious patterns which will affect me as well as those around me.

These are just some of the tools of SAT. You will find many more in the individual sessions I have included.

Structures

Dr. Wilhelm Reich [12] theorized that we are physically what we are emotionally. He saw that we carry our histories in the tissues of our body. Some of the history we know and some is hidden deep in our muscular structure and our unconscious. Dr. Alexander Lowen [2] continued Reich's work and the structures that I will be explaining are drawn from Dr. Lowen's personality structures. However, I will be giving just a short explanation of each and a very brief overview of how I work with them. If you are curious and would like more information on them I would refer you to the books on Bioenergetics by Dr Alexander Lowe [2].

These personality structures are really energy blocks or tensions armoring the body. We have formed these structures in order to protect ourselves from situations or traumas in our childhood, and sometimes in adulthood when we felt it was not safe to feel. We tightened certain areas of our bodies and formed certain behaviors, which really saved our autonomy at the time. These emotions and behaviors became embedded in our tissue and in our ways of living. We all carry most of these character structures to some extent but usually we have one or two that define our reactions to life and especially to stressful situations.

In SAT, Dick and I renamed Lowen's structures to accent the positive aspect of each as SAT really tries to focus on non-judgment and accepting myself just as I am without *trying* to change. It doesn't mean I like those aspects of myself, but rather I am aware of what I do or am feeling without judging, which opens me to change. We have found that change happens through awareness rather than effort.

When working with people, I will often notice a particular pattern or process in the way they are responding to me. This usually comes up when they are not flowing with the work. Some might call this *resistance*. I do not. I see this process as a survival technique that the child developed out of his/her genius in order to cross that dangerous river called Childhood. Probably they were scorned, punished or humiliated for it; they began to judge themselves and it has gone underground into the unconscious, where the behavior causes all sorts of problems in their lives and they are not even aware of it. Therefore, I treat this behavior with respect and gently try to help the person bring it into their conscious *awareness* by acting it out in a safe, non judgmental arena.

Often, they will end up laughing at themselves or have a sudden awareness of where this is happening in their life. Once they become conscious of the behavior and let go of their own judgement of it, they can *choose* to use the behavior at times in which they don't feel safe, and they can consciously *choose not* to use it if they do feel safe. The following is a brief explanation of the process of each structure and an example piece of work with a student.

The Creative Structure

Dr. Lowen names this Schizoid. The Creative Structure is identified more with their *thinking* than with their body. Their energy is mostly in their head and they don't have a sense of the physical support that is there for them in the amazing amount of energy of the earth. Because of this, they spend a lot of their life in fear, trusting their thinking rather than their physical sense of their body. They often are afraid of prolonged sensations in their bodies and therefore they distract themselves or interrupt their process. They have a hard time focusing on one task whether it is a direction I've given them or something they want to accomplish in their lives, or even getting out the door in time for a meeting. My main objective in working with them is to help them to trust their body, to build a tolerance for feelings (i.e. sensations and/or emotions) and to bring their energy down to their feet. When they accomplish this, they feel more secure and can live a much more focused life.

Melanie came into my office complaining that she was anxious because she could not get anything accomplished at work. Her anxiety was keeping her up at night and she felt she was grouchy at work because of this. I started to work with her breath, to bring her into bodily awareness and her energy down, out of her head. It was soon obvious that she could not keep focused for very long on the directions. She would keep interrupting to tell me something she thought was important. I asked her if she was aware of this tendency to interrupt. She was not. I then asked her to play a game with me and begin to do something (like pick up a Kleenex) and then drop it and move into another task, (like getting me a glass of water) and then stop that and move into something else so that she never completed one task. In other words, she would be interrupting herself on purpose.

After some time, she stopped and started laughing. "I just realized that I do this all the time. In fact, I have signs on my desk and on the outside of my door at work saying 'DON'T INTERRUPT ME!!' Having brought this behavior into the conscious choice, she then could work with her breath and brought herself to a place of peace. Of course, this is not a one time forever cure but a tool that needs to be practiced with awareness in order to come to a place where the unwanted behavior happens less and less.

The Lover Structure

Dr. Lowen names this Oral. The Lover Structure holds most of their energy around their heart and therefore can give themselves away in any relationship whether it is parental, work oriented, life partner, children, etc. often leaving them with resentments of these relationships without knowing why. They are in some ways the easiest to work with as they want to, and do, please you and they're usually in touch with their body sensations and emotions. However, they will comply with any direction and then sometimes feel resentful and used, just as they do in their other relationships. They need to bring their energy down to their feet, to find out what *they* want instead of what *you* want, and to take their stand in life.

Anne came to me complaining that she wanted to leave her husband whom she no longer loved and had nothing in common with. She was very unhappy and had stayed for years because of the children who were now out of the house. She wanted to leave so badly but couldn't bring herself to do it for fear of disappointing her aging parents. Her husband also opposed this move even though he ignored her and often was verbally abusive.

After having her stand with her knees bent for some time, breathing and feeling her feet, I handed her a rolled up towel. I asked her to squeeze it and repeat a sentence over and over and allow herself to experience whatever feelings came up with it. The sentence was, "Give it to me, it's mine!" Soon she was crying and yelling it with all of the pent up emotions she had held in for years. When she finished she reported feeling stronger in her body than she ever had. She later reported that she was finally able to take her stand with her husband and they were making arrangements to live separately. She also began to look at her other relationships and to realize she was very co-dependent in them. In the last few years, she has made great strides in taking care of herself rather than enmeshing herself in others' lives.

The Endurer

Dr. Lowen names this Masochist. The Endurer holds their energy in the torso, between the throat and the anus. They have incredible energy, which they usually withhold making them feel stuck in their lives and victimized. They are also very sensitive people but seldom show their feelings. Because they have a hard time saying "No', they often sabotage themselves and others by saying they will do "it" and then not *quite* doing it or by not following through. Energetically, they need to learn to allow this great reserve of energy to *flow*, letting go of negative attitudes about themselves and others.

I worked with Tom in a group setting. He started by complaining that he felt stuck in his life and that he kept procrastinating about all the things he wanted to accomplish. As we were working I became aware that he was *apparently* following all my directions and nothing was coming to completion. He was not in that place of peace or satisfaction that happens at the end of an exploration.

I asked him to do what he was already doing for the next several directions I would give him. He was confused; he didn't understand. I explained that I wanted him to *pretend* to follow my directions but to not *quite* complete them or to sabotage the experiment, and that he was to do this in a way that I might not even be able to tell that he was *not* doing as I asked. As he began to do this, going to the table and pouring me a glass of water, then adding sugar, a big smile began to spread across his face. It was fun! His behavior had come out of the unconscious and he felt very young. Then he said, "This is why my wife is always mad at me."

I then had him stamp his feet and say, "NO, I WON'T!" to all the things he didn't want to do. This left him feeling exhilarated. I advised him to do this exercise with all the projects that he was procrastinating about. When we allow ourselves the NO, it is easier to say YES.

The Challenger / Protector

Dr. Lowen names this Psychopath. The Challenger / Protector has had to use their intellect and their will to survive their childhood. Their energy is held in a tight diaphragm and in the upper part of their body and head. They are always protecting their very small, inner child because they are extremely afraid of feeling vulnerable and showing it to others; this was not safe for them as a child. Rather than feel these vulnerable feelings, they often get into either inner struggles with themselves, or outer conflicts or struggles with others.

At the same time, they are compelled to rescue or protect those they perceive as helpless or vulnerable, those being the relationships they feel comfortable in. My work with them is to help them open their heart so that they can trust

66

others. Here is a short example of a piece of SAT work with this structure, which shows the extent of the unconscious distrust.

Leo tells me he feels resistant. I ask him to say, "Cherie, you will never be as good as John" (his last therapist). He argues with me and I ask him if he will just try it as an experiment to see what happens in his body. He says the phrase with eyes closed and then says to me, "That doesn't feel right."

"That's okay," I say, "Just try it as you feel your body and see if there is a change, no matter how small. Remember this is all an experiment to find *your* truth and any change is a validation of who you are and what the truth is." Often this structure stays in their thinking and has to be reminded to watch their sensations.

He again says the phrase, "Cherie, you will never be as good as John". Now he reports feeling calmer, and decides he wants to work with me but is still intellectualizing, staying distant and in control.

I put my fists up like we are going to box. He laughs like he recognizes what he is doing. I tell him I can see by his body and his aura that he has had major abandonment issues (both parents abandon in different ways leaving the child unsafe and untrusting of their emotions and searching in their mind for answers). He agrees but still stays in his head, talking and figuring it out. I then ask him to look right into my eyes and say, "Cherie, no matter what you do, you will not *get* to me!" Again he laughs and denies that that is true. "I *want* you to get to me," he says.

I tell him I am not working with the conscious mind but rather with the mirror of the unconscious — his body. The fact that his body laughed told me there was some truth there.

Again I ask him to just say the words and *feel* his body. He looks at me again and tries it, "Cherie, no matter what you do, you will not get to me".

Again he relaxes, reporting that the calmness is back. Now having acknowledged this inner truth, he is free to move to it's opposite. He begins to trust me and lets go of this inner struggle, feeling a little safer in his body. In working with him over a period of time, he found that we had to start every session with this exercise, putting his hands into fists and pretending to fight me before we could explore the real issues. We came to characterizing it and enjoyed playing with it. In time his heart melted and he was able to see that people in general, were not out to get him.

The Achiever

Dr. Lowen names this Rigid. The Achiever appears to have it together and indeed, they are *apparently* well adjusted to our society, which rewards people who are always in control, cool and working hard to achieve. Underneath their armor though, (which they carry within their tissue), lies a lot of self doubt and self-criticism. They are often critical of others but not nearly as critical as they are of themselves. Because of the armor, i.e. hard and tense musculature, they don't allow themselves to feel much. The work here is to soften the entire body and to help them open their hearts to their own sensations of pleasure since they utilize their energy in achieving rather than feeling.

Their experience of themselves, if they are aware of their energy, is of pushing forward and holding back at the same time. One trainee could never quite get this while we were working together. Several years later, I received a letter

68

from him stating that he had an experience on an Outward Bound training where he had to grab a rope that was thrown to him and swing to the opposite tree. He had grabbed the rope, jumped and held back at the same time, and didn't make it. "I finally had the experience you were trying to get me in touch with," he wrote.

Sometimes Achievers achieve at not achieving. A young woman who had been training with me for several years, had three degrees, but could not bring herself to apply for anything more than a menial job. When working with her, I would often have her sit on the floor and push back into the wall as hard as she could. This would be quite successful in eliciting her true feelings, since a lot of the held energy in this structure is in the tense tissue in the back.

She came into my office one day very excited. She had used this same tool at home, pretending she was interviewing for the job she wanted. As she was doing this, she reported, all these good traits came tumbling out of her mouth. When she did the actual interview, she pushed back into the chair she was sitting in, felt more confident, and got the job.

The Creative Structure - Examples

The Roomy Womb

AJ came to the group complaining about her 'crazy' mother. She had worked many times before, expressing her anger at her mother for some of the things she had done while AJ was growing up and even into adulthood. I realized that she was reliving this experience of her 'young' mother and was stuck in the 'story'. I decided to do a re-taping. I asked her to lie down, close her eyes, and pretend she was back in the womb, only *this* time the womb was expansive and warm, and her mother loved her body and loved being pregnant. Every day her mother would take time to rest and feel her belly getting bigger and loving the child within. I asked her to pretend she had so much space in this womb she could roll around and stretch out to her heart's content.

AJ started to move taking a long time to stretch and soon she was rocking. This was all done in silence and after quite some time, she sat up and said she felt great. She looked wonderful with a softness and a lot of color in her face.

I often give this body fantasy (meaning that I ask the person to feel the fantasy in their body rather than just visualizing) to what I call the Creative Personality Structure. This is the child who was traumatized in utero by the mother (who carried a lot of fear and tightness in her pelvis — therefore a tight womb).

The next month AJ returned to the group saying that that piece of work had been life changing for her. The rocking had stayed with her for a long time and she felt more solid and peaceful. She again wanted to work on her mother whom she felt closer to than she ever had, and was at that time in the hospital in ICU.

As she talked to her mother, for the first time in our work together her love surfaced. She began to cry, saying, "I don't know what I will do when you are gone. You gave me so much. The world will not be the same without you." She continued expressing her love and her grief. When she was finished, the group was amazed at her coloring. She looked radiant. It reminded me that after a workshop, someone had once sent me a picture of a sign on a building stating, CHERIE'S BEAUTY SHOP.

This piece of work brings to mind the work of Desmond Tutu [15] and his book, *The Book of Forgiving*. In it he describes the steps toward healing myself of traumas (which is what forgiveness does). They are:

1. Tell the story
2. Feel the emotion of the trauma
3. Forgive the other
4. Renew or eliminate the relationship

When this has been accomplished, and it may take a long time and many visits to these four steps, you get the rewards. There are always gifts that come from our traumas, if we look for them, but we seldom see them until we have gone through these steps. Each time a person goes through this series, they lighten the load of resentment that is poisoning them.

As a great being once said, "Hatred is like eating poison and expecting the other person to die."

The Perky Grandma

She reported the first day of the workshop that she had been depressed since the accident. She had been hit by a car and knocked off her bike, breaking her nose and injuring her leg. Her eight year old grandson who had been riding behind her was hysterically yelling, "You hit my Grandma! You hit my Grandma!". When the police arrived, she had defended the driver. This did not surprise me as we had worked before on her co dependency. Always feeling sorry for the underdog and putting others before herself, she saw that the young man was probably here illegally and tried to rescue him. When the police arrived, she took his side.

Having repressed her anger, she was terrified to have the operation on her broken nose and lapsed into depression. She nevertheless had that operation but was still suffering from residual pain, physical and emotional.

She came into the center of the circle to explore all this and I asked her to close her eyes, focus into her body and tell me her sensations. She had a hard time with this task and it was obvious that she was stuck in her thinking, still rationalizing the young man's actions and interrupting herself. This interrupting is typical of the personality structure I call the Creative, who has a hard time staying focused. I usually work with an unconscious defense like this before I go on with a person, asking them to do what they are doing on purpose. This brings the behavior out if the unconscious where it is happening compulsively, into the conscious choice. When the person acts out their compulsive behavior with awareness, the compulsion let's go for a while. Gradually, using this technique again and again, the person becomes more and more aware, giving them freedom from the behavior, or in this case, an ability to be more focused.

I gave her a rolled up towel, asked her to squeeze it and talk to the young driver. Again she began to interrupt. I asked her to interrupt on purpose, to begin to squeeze the towel and then stop and tell me something. After doing this several times, her anger emerged. She told him she was angry that he had given false information to the police.

I then asked her to say, "You frightened my grandson!" (I often give a sentence to say as an experiment to see what changes in the body. The body being 'the mirror' of the unconscious, will often respond where the mind denies). She repeated the sentence.

Suddenly she was *very* angry. "Nobody scares my grandson!" she screamed over and over. Soon she was also screaming, "YOU BROKE MY NOSE!! YOU BROKE MY NOSE!!"

Having released the anger, she began breathing quietly with deep belly breaths. She looked soft, relaxed and younger, the lines in her face evened out. She reported feeling "pretty good".

The next morning as we were relating how our evenings were spent, she told the group that her grandson had been with her for the evening. She commented that at one point he had said, "I've got my perky grandma back!"

This demonstrates how change can happen when an unconscious truth is spoken, in this case, "Nobody scares my grandson". You may have had the experience of feeling tingles when someone else says something that feels true to you. This is the same phenomenon.

Another example of anger turned to depression is the young teacher who came into my office many years ago, complaining that depression had landed her in the hospital every spring. Again, remember that depression is low energy, low self esteem and lack of movement. I handed her a jump rope and asked her to jump. This was very hard for her at first, as she kept interrupting her jumping to tell me more of the story. When she could finally continue the jumping for a bit, I asked her to chant, "I'm angry, I'm angry, I'm angry," as she was jumping. She began again and after awhile had to rest for a few moments. Then I instructed her to jump again and say all the things she was angry about.

"I'm angry that I have to get up every day and go to that school. I'm angry at those kids! I'm angry that I have so many papers to correct! Night after night after night," she yelled, "I can't keep up. I'm overwhelmed. I hate it!" She went on and on.

After she finished, she reported feeling relief and pleasurable sensations in her body. I told her to take the jump rope home and practice and come back next week.

The next week she reported feeling much better and in the following weeks we worked in more detail with her anger.

The next year she sent me a note saying she had not gone into her spring depression, had not had her annual visit to the hospital and that she was still using her jump rope instead.

I often use a pretend jump rope if one isn't handy or the ceiling is low. Just moving the arms in a circle and jumping will allow more breath into the lungs and get energy moving in both the upper and lower body. That along with expressing what the person is angry about will bring about a change in attitude and a sense of well being.

The Lover Structure - Example

I Am Unlovable

Joanne lay on the floor, crying about the latest breakup with her boyfriend, realizing that she had again caused it. Suddenly I asked her to stand up, to come close to me and look me in the eyes. I really wanted to connect with her and told her this. When she did this I asked her to look at me and say "I am unloveable".

Her eyes widened in fear and she covered them. She couldn't say it. I waited, knowing that she was feeling the truth of my words in her body. Soon she whispered, "I have to walk around", and she walked into the adjoining room for a bit. I waited, allowing her to decide if she wanted to explore this very scary space within. She had done a lot of work with me and had learned to trust her body's truth, so I waited.

When she came back, she said, "This is so scary!"

"Can you be scared and still do it?", I asked.

"Yes," she answered. Her eyes were still wide and full of tears as she stepped close to me and whispered, "I am unlovable." She then went around the room repeating the words as she made close contact with each person, looking directly into their eyes. When she finished, she sat down in the middle of the group and closed her eyes, breathing.

Suddenly a big smile broke across her face and she exclaimed, "I've never felt this good. I feel tingly all over." I asked her to lie flat and let herself just take it in, to let her tissue memorize this place. Like the athlete or dancer who performs the same movements over and over creating muscle memory, each time we go into that place of peace and/or pleasure, we are creating tissue memory. I always respect that space and give a suggestion, a reminder that the body is memorizing. After a bit she reported feeling a deep peace. I asked her to feel it and say, "This is who I *really* am."

"This is who I *really* am, this is who I *really* am," she repeated over and over until she fell into a quiet space. We all sat and witnessed until she asked for feedback.

Later she told me that she now realized that she had always felt unlovable, had been fighting the feeling all her life and it was such a relief to accept it, i.e. to let herself really experience it. By letting yourself feel the deepest most fearful experience, the polarity arises, like the Phoenix from the fire. In this case, to really let herself feel unlovable, she finally swung to its opposite which is loving herself. This is the gift of Self Acceptance.

This unconscious and sometimes conscious feeling of being unlovable is a very common experience of the Lover Personality Structure. Having some experience of abandonment as a child, they tend to see it often in everyday happenings, recreating the terrible loss of love in their primary relationships.

Polly wanted to work on how she had been placed in an orphanage at birth where she remained for six weeks. She never left the fetal position and had refused to eat. After being adopted, her very loving parents would set a clock, wake up for her feeding time and wait with warm bottled milk for her to awaken. They had a lot of love and swaddled her in it. However, that early abandonment had left its scars.

She came to me complaining about her present relationship where she felt she never got enough. He had told her he couldn't give anymore and she felt angry. I had her lie on the floor and raise her hands, reaching and calling out "I want MORE!" over and over. Louder and louder. The need for exaggerated sound is important in this work as it allows more energy to be discharged. She soon was sobbing uncontrollably. At this point she had been talking to her partner.

When she calmed a bit, I asked her to go back into the exercise. This time when she began to yell "MORE, MORE, I NEED MORE!!" I asked her to say that to her birth mother. She stopped for a few seconds, stunned, and then whimpered "I need you". She again sobbed, this time for quite a while. (She later said she felt very young). I waited for her to quiet down and soon saw her taking deep belly breaths. Her whole aura changed and a calm came over the room. When people come to this calm, peaceful place, I realize they are in an altered state and I am quiet and wait for as long as it takes for them to come out of it. I truly believe they are learning things at a deeper unconscious level that I could never teach them.

After a bit of time she mumbled something and I asked her what she said, "I just said to Bob, "I'm okay, I really feel strong!" She then turned to me and said, "You know, I always felt if I let myself really experience that sadness of being abandoned, I wouldn't ever stop. But it's just the opposite, I feel stronger after feeling it!"

This is a very common fear in our culture where most people have been taught to tighten different parts of their bodies in order to control their emotions. These tensions can become chronic creating many problems. What a wonderful lesson she learned here, that the organism is self regulating.

This personality structure (the Lover Structure) has experienced early abandonment, and has been scarred in the sucking stage of development, has a great need to be loved and never quite feels loved. They also have a great capacity to love others and often feel like they have no place or no one to give that love to.

As I have some of this structure in my own makeup, I have experienced these feelings myself and found, just as this young woman, that it really helps to allow those feelings in their intensity and that, just like a bell that swings all the way to the top of its arc in one direction, it soon comes to the other side of its swing — from total helplessness to wonderful strength.

Another tool that I have learned to alleviate the awful need to love when there is no one to love is calling out to God (or whatever higher power or belief of the divine that you have — it could be 'nature'), "I LOVE YOU! I LOVE YOU!! I LOVE YOU!!! over and over until the feeling is quenched). Believe it or not this is a wonderful tool for the Lover Structure. Without the awareness of this powerful need, the lover structure can become love addicted to the wrong person and/or can become codependent, seeking that love in dysfunctional relationships.

The Endurer Structure - Example

The Underground No

Jerry was not there on Saturday, the first day of the workshop. This was a concern to me, as he had been working with me for a few years and was very reliable. When I called him at the break, he said his depression was so bad that he couldn't get out of bed. He promised me he would be there on Sunday.

I knew he was prone to depression but he still had never missed a workshop. His depression covered rage at the universe, i.e. God, and at himself. He had been addicted to drugs at a very early age and it had stunted his self confidence. He had lost his job and was living at home with his parents who were very aged and unhealthy. He would soon find himself alone. I knew this was terrifying him. At this time he had little income and his parents were not financially well off.

On Sunday, he arrived looking withdrawn and very depressed. I decided to work with him first. Depression is often repressed anger, low self esteem (identifying with self judgement instead of the body), minimal movement, and minimal breathing. I decided to use Dr. Alexander Lowen's [2] Bioenergetic exercises, which take the student back to childlike ways of expressing. I had him do charging-discharging three times to get his energy moving. This exercise puts the body in a non-painful stress position in which the front and then the back of the body is placed in a posture of self regulated traction. With deep breathing and the use of loud sound the person begins to get energy moving while stretching and relaxing the tissue. After asking his permission, I began lightly tapping his back, reminding the tissue to let go.

After doing this for several minutes his legs began to shake. This was evidence that his energy was traveling down his legs and into his feet. I then asked him to stand and put his attention in his feet saying, "The earth is my support", then to take a deep breath feeling his lungs and say, "The air is my support". He repeated this over and over, paying attention to the sensations of his breath and his connection to his feet.

Done this way, this mantra reminds the person that our real support is in the "holy mystery", the energy of the body, the air and the earth. To get caught up in the *belief* that support is outside of me is to live in fear of losing it, and indeed all those things which we label 'our support' can be gone tomorrow. Money, degrees, home, loved ones, all can be lost. When the energy moves down, out of the head, people often report feeling more secure, more self confident and whole. The concept seems strange until you actually experience it. I often explain that as everything is energy, the earth is the largest object of energy in the near vicinity, and when the energy which is the body actually becomes concentrated in the feet, the earth acts like a strong magnet which can be felt as security. Suddenly, the person feels like he/she can handle whatever is happening in life, they feel their inner strength. This is what some people call *'grounding'*.

I asked him how he was feeling. His reply was, "Pretty good--alive!"

I then asked him to lie down, with his knees bent so his feet could be flat. When he had done that I asked him to start

80

beating his flat feet and flat hands in what Dr. Lowen [2] calls a *temper tantrum*. Because he had done this before, he knew to use his voice, yelling, "NOOOOOO". All of his rage was soon spilling out. "NOOOO. I WANT ABUNDANCE!!! I WANT SELF CONFIDENCE!!! NOOOO TO ALL OF THIS. NOOOOOOO!!!!! Now he was releasing all of his repressed rage that had kept him in bed, depressed.

Soon, he was lying quietly, breathing deeply into his belly, the movement flowing all the way down the front of his body and even into his legs. He reported feeling strong and very pleasurable.

The Endurer Structure has repressed their rage and often turn it against themselves, sabotaging themselves in life experiences and at times falling into depression.

The Challenger / Protector Structure - Example

Tolerating Vulnerability

Sonya had worked with me several times before but had a really hard time allowing herself to become vulnerable. Usually her sessions would consist of what some people would call resistance. I call it the Challenger/Protector, a defense that the child has developed in order to save their autonomy. I do not judge it as it was the child's friend and I try to help the person to stop judging it so they can use it when they need it, be aware of it when it arises, and then set it aside so it does not run their lives. I see this person with one hand reaching out pleading, "Please help me," and the other hand pushing away, not trusting, expecting that I will somehow take away their *choice* and control them. The main work with this person is to help them to trust their body, that the body has their truth and that they have choice.

So most of the work with Sonya would usually culminate with me catching her not doing what I asked her to do and her laughing at herself. Many times I would ask her to say, "Cherie, You're not gonna get to me," and then she would laugh. This was her inner truth and again, I never judged her or tried to change her. It was enough for her to learn to be aware.

This particular day she had come in feeling really sad and saying she just wanted to be alone. The fact that she was there and had come to the group showed me her progress because this personality would normally go off by themselves when they felt like this. You could see that she was feeling very vulnerable when she came into the center of the group to work.

I acknowledged that for her, pointing out that she had made the choice to come into the center even though she was scared, and she could also make the *choice* to go into those feelings and express them or she could also *choose* to repress them. Either way, it was her *choice* and it was okay. "I always turn them off," she said.

I pointed out that I could still see the sadness in her face and in her eyes, again acknowledging her. I could see she was fighting it. I took a chance and asked her to close her eyes and just feel it. She did this and I sat with that for a bit. Then I said, "You could *choose* to open your mouth and make a tiny sound. I again sat in silence waiting to see what she would do. Again, I could see her fighting with herself. Finally, she let out a little sound, then a little more and a little more. Tears were flowing. Suddenly, she opened her eyes, smiled through her tears and said. "I just turn it off."

I smiled at her and said, "Sonya, you just did a wonderful piece of work, you allowed yourself to be vulnerable in front of all of us and you can choose to deny it, but that is coming from your head. How do you feel in your body?".

"I feel softer.", she said. The group then gave her feedback, saying she looked radiant, which she did.

Because this structure was so controlled in their childhood, they lost their sense of choice and realized it was not safe to feel vulnerable. Therefore the main thrust as I work with them is to help them learn to tolerate their own vulnerability. In order to accomplish this, I have to stay 100% free of ego investment, allowing them to see that whatever they *choose* to do is *their* choice. If they *choose* to follow my directions, it is their choice. If they *choose* to do something else, it is their choice. Once they have learned *that*, they can begin to tolerate their feelings because they realize *they* are in control, not me. Then, little by little, they learn to go deeper into themselves, discovering their own inner truths.

Here is another example of the Challenger / Protector Structure and how their fear of vulnerability in relationships brings them into a struggle within themselves. This inner conflict often results in fantasizing about or having other relationships besides the *main* one or by waffling in and out. To truly *love someone is to be vulnerable.* One of the sentences I often give them to say to the loved one is, "If I let myself love you, I'm afraid you will control me.", as this expresses the original, unconscious struggle with the parent.

Bobbi came to me, complaining that she kept changing her mind about this current relationship. She just couldn't commit. Because she had been training with me for a number of years, she knew this was not about her boyfriend but about her own fears. Still, she was troubled. She was sitting on a three by five foot blanket on the carpeted floor. I asked her to stand up and walk around the blanket with one foot on the blanket and the other on the floor saying, "I'm in. I'm out. I'm in. I'm out." She did this for a while, laughing at herself, then getting frustrated. "But what can I do?" She really wanted to change.

"You need to love and accept yourself just as you are," I said. "This is an important part of you and as long as you stay aware of it, you can let it go when it doesn't serve you and use it when it does. All change begins with *awareness.* If you can let go of the judgement of it, allow yourself to experience the

84

struggle, knowing that the feeling is about something in your past, not necessarily about the present, then it will let go for a time. Gradually, you will experience it less and less. Use the tools"

"How do I do that with my boyfriend?"

"Well, how do you feel about him right now?" I asked.

"I don't know. It's a struggle." She stamped her foot. She had slipped back into her head about it and back into the struggle.

"Yes," I said, "Stamp your feet. Keep stomping — and as you're stomping, chant 'Struggle, struggle, struggle'." She began doing this and continued until she was laughing at herself again. She was back in the experience of acceptance.

"You see," I said, "You just allowed yourself to experience your struggle without judging it or trying to change it. This is Self Acceptance. You can do this dance whenever you get into the 'struggle' space. And each time you come into this place you are in now, your body will be memorizing and remembering that it is safe. It is safe to just be who you are."

I always underline a person's work with positive truths or intentions or suggestions because we all need to be validated, especially when we are in that open hearted state. The next morning she whispered to me, "I'm feeling so much love in my heart for him."

The Achiever Structure - Examples

The "D" Word

Elaine wanted to work on her marriage. She was very unhappy and had stayed for twenty-three years (for the kids), and felt like it was killing her! I asked her to talk to her husband. She began by telling him how miserable she had been for years and all the details of why. He had been absent in so many ways and had turned the boys against her. She went on and on. Finally she said, "I want...."

She looked at me and said, "I can't say it."

"What?" I asked.

"You know, the D word."

She had worked with me five years ago and come to the same place. I hadn't seen her since. She had decided to wait 'til the boys had finished college'. This often happens with the personality structure I call the Achiever. They have a hard time allowing themselves to *want their pleasure* and get stuck in performance (in this case, motherhood and being a good wife).

I knew that her mother had divorced her father and she felt that it had ruined the family. She had worked on that the day before and had come to a very good place with forgiving her mother, realizing that her mother had been in a very similar place to where she found herself now, feeling that there was no love for her in the marriage. Still, she could not bring herself to say the word, divorce. *Refer to chapter on Tools (Stepping*

86

into Someone Else's Shoes). "It is just a word," I said. I began to chant the word. "Di-vorce, Di-vorce, Di-vorce." I began to clap my hands. Soon the group joined me. We were all chanting and clapping. Suddenly, Elaine began to chant. She jumped up and began dancing, chanting as she moved. She danced 'til she dropped, laughing. Then she stood up and said, "I want a DIVORCE!!!

"YEAH!!", the group yelled.

When I started to chant, I had no idea where it would go. She could have cried or gotten angry or had other responses. In those situations I go with my intuition and trust that whatever comes up, we will deal with.

An after note: It still took Elaine a bit of time before she was able to tell her husband, first telling him she wanted to move on her own to another state, and then, finally, telling him she wanted a divorce. I always respect a person's own timing for change.

The Blocked Heart

David claims he is afraid to get involved with women and yet he wants to. He says he has never loved anyone. When asked if he had loved his wife whom he had divorced many years ago, he replies, "Probably not." I ask him to close his eyes and tell me what he is feeling in his body. "My chest feels numb." he says. I notice his breath does not come into his upper chest. "It feels like Styrofoam," he says. I ask him to breathe into it and drift back to times in his life where he had to block his love because he had been hurt.

He goes back through several dating experiences where he had not felt anything, making excuses why 'this' woman was not for him, that one was not right, obviously feeling his heart closed.   Suddenly he was back in his marriage. "I feel something," he says. "It hurts."   This tells me he is starting to let go. I ask him to breathe into it and talk to her. "I guess I did love you sometimes." He starts to talk to his ex-wife and the more he remembers, the softer he becomes, the more his breathing comes up into his heart area.   His energy is moving.   He says, "It was the happiest time of my life," and he starts to cry. He sobs more, and softens. "This is scary," he says.

"Yes," I say,   "A great being once said, *'The most courageous thing we can do is to soften.'*   Is it scary and painful, or scary and pleasurable?"

"Pleasurable," was the reply. "Did you ever tell her that you loved her?" I ask.

"No."

"Go back to some specific times and tell her."

"We're riding bikes around the bay and you look so happy riding in front of me. I love you." He starts to sob again. This goes on for several minutes, him telling her times when he felt his love. Then he says, "That's probably why she left me. I never told her."

This piece of work demonstrates what I call the Achiever Structure Personality and shows how a person who has blocked their heart (usually in childhood) may not be conscious even when their heart opens, not acknowledging their feelings to themselves or to the loved one. The hardest part of this scenario is to realize that when we say "I love you," we are validating ourselves. When we voice any of our feelings we validate our self. This is a crucial component in being a whole human being. We know how important validation is in parenting. The child who comes in with a skinned knee does not want the parent to say, "I'll get a bandaid," or "I told you not to ride your bike on the gravel." They want the parent to validate where they are at, what they are feeling. "Ohhh, you hurt yourself." And the child relaxes.

We all want and need validation from others and this need never ends. However, even more important, we need to validate ourselves and we do that by feeling our body sensations and emotions and stating them to ourselves and to others. When we do that, we come in touch with our inner truth, our inner healer.

This piece of work also brings to mind how people sometimes have a hard time knowing what I'm looking for when I ask if it is pleasure or pain. They do not realize that every sensation in the body is pleasure or pain. Our culture tends to ignore sensations until they become extreme. I often hold my hand in a fist to explain that held tight for a long time I will bring about pain, i.e. energy trying to move. After a while, if I continue to hold it like that, I will feel numb, just like David felt in his chest. If I begin to open my fist the first thing I will feel is pain. Again energy trying to move. After the pain goes away I will feel what most people call "normal" sensations. I call this pleasure because energy is moving. Even though most of our bodily experiences are made up of these "normal" sensations most people dismiss them, waiting for extreme pleasure. I spend a lot of time teaching students that energy moving is a pleasurable experience no matter how slight. When they really get this concept, they become more aware of their bodies and find a lot more pleasure in their life.

Love, Hate, Resentment and Guilt

Some people ask, "What about love and hate?" Although these can elicit all kinds of sensations in the body as well as emotions, they are attitudes. An attitude can color my responses in many ways. For instance, if I love someone, I may feel fear, joy, anger or sadness in connection with that person. The attitude of hate is often experienced as extreme anger or fear and acted out in a variety of behaviors. what most people do do understand is that the absence of love is not hate (you can love and hate the same person). The absence of love is indifference.

Attitudes of guilt and shame are both forms of self-hatred. Although we usually lump these together, they are quite different. Guilt is the polarity of resentment. It is resentment at someone else which I have turned at myself and then I am the one who suffers from my own anger. It is important to remember that when you are in guilt, you make yourself a victim and will be feeling miserable. When you move to resentment, you come into your strength. When you can let go of the resentment after feeling it you will be in peace.

An example from my own life was in my care taking of my stepfather whom I loved very much. I was seeing him about three or four times a week and feeling so guilty that I didn't spend more time with him. I felt this awful sensation in my body. He was suffering from Alzheimer's and didn't communicate much. When I realized how much I was suffering from this guilt, I used the Gestalt technique of talking out loud to his children (who weren't really there). "You are totally neglectful of him. I am so resentful that I have all the responsibility and everything is on my shoulders." I then discovered that I had resentments even at him for leaving me and slipping into Alzheimer's (emotions, you see, are not rational).

After speaking to him as if he were there, telling him how angry I was that he had gotten this terrible disease and abandoned me, I found my attitude of guilt had abated. I found myself feeling the loss and the love that felt so good to me and that he really deserved. He didn't have to know that I was angry at him, his children didn't have to know that I was angry at them, but I needed to *express* my inner truth. Once that was done, nothing changed in the outer circumstances but my inner climate was clear. I was able to go back to my care taking with the love and commitment that I wanted to feel in this incredible and fulfilling journey with him.

Dr. Fritz Perls [13] used to have his own Golden Rule in his Gestalt Therapy. "Do unto others what you do to yourself". Of course he didn't mean this literally. He meant if you were angry with yourself, you probably had turned the anger you had at someone else toward yourself, and you would feel better if you expressed it, pretending the person was there. He called this the *I-Thou* experience.

Often we bury our resentments in our bodies. My mother, who felt guilty about a number of things in her life, suffered from arthritis. Periodically she would spend several days in bed with back pain. She had been kicked in the lower back as a child and suffered physical abuse from my father for five years of their early marriage. During one of these bouts in

91

bed, I gave her Fritz Perls' book, *In And Out The Garbage Pail* [13]. She came across this passage:

"I would ask each member of the group to say a sentence starting with: "I resent" – then follow up with a fantasy encounter with that person until the resentment was resolved."

As she read this, she realized she was very angry with her boss at a small school for developmentally challenged children, who did not like a woman driving a bus. He told her if she could take a man's job and drive a school bus, then she could lift the heavy garage door to get the bus in and out of the garage.   In doing that, she had injured her back again and found herself in this situation. She started talking to him as she lay there in bed.   Soon she was yelling at him and then she started kicking the bed and thrashing with her fists.

Although she had never worked with me, she had heard me telling of the healing effect Dr. Lowen's [2] temper tantrum had and her body had automatically gone into this exercise. Suddenly she realized she had no pain. She got up and never spent another day in bed.   She had used Fritz Perl's Golden Rule *"Do onto others what you are doing to yourself"* and changed her life. She had been kicking herself in the back with her anger and instead, kicked the bed, i.e her boss.

Shame is an attitude about something that we have done or something someone else has done to us, in which there is self-judgment, and we want to hide it from the world. We start to identify with the action and on some level we believe it is who we are. This can be a physical action or it can be a belief that someone has infused into our consciousness with verbal abuse. The more we hide it, the more it festers, like a thorn under a saddle. It often gives us a *wild ride* in our nagging minds. We feel shame. The way to absolve it is to tell as many people as we can. I often say "Shout it from the rooftops." It is important, of course, to choose people who will not judge us for this, people who are open enough to know that we are all human, learning from our mistakes.

One young woman I was working with for a number of years in my groups finally felt safe to tell the group that she had trafficked drugs as a young girl, how scary it was and how awful she felt about it. She was now an upstanding citizen, living a useful and productive life after struggling to clean up her addictions. However she was plagued with shame about this period of her life and the things she had done in order to survive in that life. After going to each person in the group, looking them in the eyes and telling each one the details of her shame, using the phrase, "I am ashamed that I....", she felt great relief.

Many years later she told me that this piece of work had saved her life. She was living shame free. She had really experienced the sensations and emotions in the group that day as she looked into each person's eyes and then she was able to let it go. It really was in her past and she felt alive in her present life.

A doctor, one evening in an ongoing group, confessed that he was a heroin addict. He was ashamed, that he had tried to quit several times on his own, had gone through the terrible withdrawal several times by himself, lonely and miserable and then gone back to it time and again. After telling each person, while looking them straight in the eyes, he announced that he now felt he could reach out for help, go into rehab and let others know about his problem.

An elderly lady who came for private counseling finally confessed to me that she had been raped as a young child. She had so much shame around it, thinking that she had brought it on because she liked this person. I encouraged her to come into one of my groups because I knew it would be a very accepting atmosphere. When she went around, telling her story, she saw so much compassion. Suddenly she turned to me and said, "It really wasn't my fault!" In that moment the attitude of shame and the underlying self-judgment and identification with the action had vanished.

She continued to come to the group and worked on many other situations that were haunting her. One day she exclaimed, "The more I let go of my past, the younger I am. Whoopee!"

Finding The I-Thou Experience

Talking about or talking to

Many people are uncomfortable feeling sensations and emotions. This is often the result of training in the family. There are many ways the message is conveyed to the child.

Sometimes through physical or verbal abuse, sometimes by witnessing violence, or sometimes with just a quiet angry look or gesture. Often children who have painful medical procedures or encounters will get the message that it is not safe to feel their body. The child then learns it is safer to stay in the intellect, numbing the emotions and tucking them, as tension, into the tissues of the body. I often have to retrain clients to experience these sensations and emotions.

That is why I prefer working in groups as the group works as an accepting, loving family who demonstrate that emotions (even extreme emotions at times) can be experienced with out violence, hurting someone's feelings, or acting out. It also demonstrates that intense emotions are not to be feared and can make dramatic change in a person's body and life.

Alex had originally come to me with an extremely tight body and had a hard time giving people hugs at the end of the workshop. He was much more comfortable talking *'about'* his parents and his horrific childhood, telling us that his father had been a criminal and had done violent and illegal things to people. I had explained to him many times that talking *'about'* kept him safely in his head where he could leak a few tears occasionally but his body remained tense. When *talking about* or leaking a few tears, people feel a slight release of tension, and often get addicted to the **story** and feel compelled to tell it over and over. The real healing would come, I explained, when he could talk *to* his parents because that would bring him into an 'I-Thou' experience which would bring up feelings in his body, releasing tensions and old traumas from the tissue, discharging or moving the energy, thus bringing about change in his life. Of course, feelings were terrifying to him and he had lived most of his life in his mind.

Sitting in groups over a period of time, with people who were so accepting of him, just as he was, and modeling for him that he could go into intense experiences and come away feeling pleasure and cleansed and free, finally gave him the courage to try it.

He addressed his father. "You terrified me with your guns and knives and threats, trying to control everybody. And you treated me like a possession, not a human but someone you could mold into what you wanted me to be, a GANGSTER!!!. You wanted me to be tough, like you." "BUT I WASN'T TOUGH LIKE YOU!!!", he yelled again and again.

Lying on the floor, he began to pound his feet and hands as he had seen others do, as he continued to yell at his father. Then he started to sob.

Finally, he became calm, his breath moving his entire torso. We waited for him as this quiet time at the end of an intense experience is so important. I have often told students that this is the time when your tissue is memorizing a new way of being. This softness is being held and memorized just as the tension was memorized when you were young and in that traumatic time.

At last he opened his eyes, smiled at me and said, "I feel pretty good!"

People were amazed at how soft and young he looked. After that, he really enjoyed saying goodbye with a hug. Alex continued to come to weekend groups and continued to soften in his body and feel more free in his life.

Mermaid in a Bubble

All of life exists in waves. The oceans, the seasons and even breath have this undulating pattern of contact and withdrawal. Life is energy and energy comes in waves. When you are hooked up to an electrocardiogram machine for an EKG, that also prints out in waves, you don't want to see it flatline which means that the heart has stopped. The energy waves or vibration of energy is very important to life and to physical and emotional health.

In my work, as in Dr. Alexander Lowen's Bioenergetics, [2] I am always watching this vibration of energy in the body. I am watching for what is called a *streaming of energy*, which can be seen sometimes as a very subtle shaking, or sometimes a lot of shaking, and sometimes only in the aura. When this shaking happens in the body, the person often gets scared since we are taught that this is an out of control reaction. However, if I can get that person to focus on the sensation instead of what the mind is calling it, he/she feels pleasurable and often has a profound sense of connection to all of life. This connection is one of the main goals of Self Acceptance Training. This connection to all of life is also the natural way of being and as earlier peoples did, how we could be experiencing every moment.

Unfortunately, in our stress filled culture we tense the body creating energy blocks so our energy does not flow freely. This is experienced as cold spots, hot spots, aches, pains, discomfort and sometimes disease. Also, for the most part in our culture, we are taught to ignore the energy flow in our bodies and instead, to value and develop our thinking abilities.

It is a good thing to develop the mind. After all, the mind is our crowning glory and differentiates us from other animals. The problem happens when we get so caught up in our thinking that we forget that we are a body. Sometimes we tense our bodies so much it's almost impossible to allow the body to shake or sob if that is what it needs. This is true for many people.

Often, people, who throughout their lives have tensed their bodies in order to protect themselves from hurt, have tightened the tissue around the heart and the diaphragm. When hurt comes to them now, they can only experience anger. Anger is a secondary emotion, often experienced in defense of vulnerability and hurt, which is a primary emotion. Here is a session that exemplifies all of these things.

Sarah came to me labeling herself an angry person, and saying everyone looks down on her because she's angry. She tells me therapists have not helped her because they have encouraged her anger, only making her life more miserable. She believes that no one likes her and those closest to her don't really love her. She is caught in her thinking which is mostly negative and we have been working on changing her attitude and reining in her thoughts, bringing the energy out of her head and down into her feet. Her diaphragm is very tight and because of this, most of her energy and awareness is up in her head and not in her feet. Besides feeling very vulnerable around people, she has a lot of fears, all of which she turns into anger.

When our energy is not flowing into our feet, we feel like we can't cope and our lives will be filled with fear. In other words we are caught in our thinking. Conversely, when the energy is flowing downward, we feel our feet and feel we can cope with the most amazing outer circumstances from a truly calm and confident place within ourselves, trusting that all will be well.

Sarah comes into my office saying she wants to work on a dream, in which her sister is very angry at her. After talking about her sister a bit, her own anger begins to escalate. I remind her that there is really fear behind this. She suddenly announces that she's afraid her children don't love her and that her daughter is more connected to her sister than to her.

Soon she is sobbing in earnest. It goes on for a time and then subsides. She reports feeling much better and her stomach is making rumbling noises, (a sign that the energy is moving down toward the feet). I then ask her if she wants to work on the dream. I use mostly Gestalt dream work developed by Dr. Fritz Perls in which the belief is that everything in the dream is a part of ourselves that we have denied and tossed into the unconscious [19].

The technique is to *feel* yourself back in the dream and re-identify with each object and each person by saying, for instance, "I am this highway and I go on and on. People use me to get places. I am sturdy and can handle lots of traffic. etc." (As I'm just writing this I realize that I'm talking about my work and my private life in which I am doing a lot of service for people. I sometimes forget that I am sturdy, have a lot of energy and actually enjoy helping people. Just this little bit gives me a more positive outlook and attitude right now as I've been feeling a little burned out in caring for my step father who has Alzheimer's.)

In Sarah's dream, she is looking for a lost statue. Her sister is in the room and starts to make mean remarks. Sarah becomes so angry she calls her a rich bitch. She leaves the room and she sees a mermaid in a bubble behind the door. That's the end of the dream.

I ask her to close her eyes, go back into the dream and wait until she really feels herself there, then begin to talk as her sister Jo. She begins,"I am Jo. I'm very artistic, I'm strong and I have friends. I am free." I ask her to repeat the last sentence a couple times and then ask her to tell me how *she* is feeling. She reports feeling very good and that those are her traits too, which she has not always felt confident about, especially in Jo's shadow.

Then I ask her to be the mermaid. She continues, "I am this mermaid. I am voluptuous and sensuous and I'm floating in this bubble. I'm safe in this bubble." She interrupted herself and started to judge herself for being in a bubble. "I'm really trapped", she said. I reminded her that judgments like that come from the mind and asked her to go back and be the mermaid again and just be in the bubble. Suddenly she was in the bubble and floating. When she let herself feel the floating, it was actually quite pleasant. I asked her to tell me her sensations and she replied that she felt a spiraling through her whole body, she could feel her belly button, and a pleasant tingling. She felt her blood circulating and that was quite astonishing, as she had begun to have trouble with her circulation lately. I told her to just lie there and feel that for as long as she wanted.

An update: After working with Sarah regularly for a few years there is such a difference in her inner experience. Not only has she allowed herself to soften and let go of most of her anger, but she has healed her relationships with her aging mother, her sister and her co-workers.

Recently, she reported that she had talked separately to her mother and her sister, who did not get along, had arranged for them to talk on the phone and then to have some private time in person. I asked what she was feeling in her body as she told me this and she said, "A lot of sensation in my right leg." Since the right side of the body signifies mother or women issues in the body (this comes out of Chinese medicine),[16] I asked her to talk to her mother.

"I don't know how long you are going to be around and I really want to heal what's happened in our family. I know Jo needs to heal too." She went on like this.

"What are you feeling now?" I asked. "My feet are tingling," was the reply. This was so gratifying to me because she had come to me so terrified of her vulnerability and so focused in her thinking, had worked so hard and changed so much that now her energy was flowing in most of our sessions.

"I want to talk to my brother," she said. She continued, "John, you have misused the family money. Our sense of family is lost, everyone is at odds." She paused. "I have come to accept it. I have learned to love." I asked her to repeat this last phrase many times and to feel the words in her body.

She reported energy flowing down her arms and out her hands. I reminded her that the arms and hands are the work organ for the heart chakra. I teach my students about the work and sense organs of each of the chakras. The hands being where we send energy out of the heart, the skin being the

102

sense organ where we bring energy into the heart. When you think of the skin being the largest organ of the body and how little we get touched, you realize how we are all starving for love.

Pleasure

She came late for her appointment, saying she had a chaotic day and needed to be out in half an hour. I said that would be no problem as she went into her body faster than most. I asked her to lie on the mat, close her eyes and scan her body. With her eyes closed she proceeded to tell me how her life had changed since she had been seeing me. She had stopped trying to fix everyone, had used a lot of the tools for releasing her anger in a healthy way, and had been allowing herself to cry. She said her relationships with her children and husband had improved.

I reminded her to breathe, to come into the now and asked what she was feeling "The only sensation I have is in my lower back. It's not painful," she said in a curious voice.

"Well, If it's not pain, it's pleasure," I reminded her. (So much of the time, we dismiss small sensations, waiting for extreme feelings).

"Yes," she said, "It is pleasurable."

"Dick Olney always said, 'Self Acceptance is too good to use only when we are in pain. The best time to use the tools is when we are in pleasure'," I told her.

"Wow, yes, I feel pleasure. So what do I do with it?" she asked. "Breathe into it and say all the things in your life right now that bring you pleasure." I said. "Let the words *be* the sensations."

"I have pleasure hiking with my son and sitting at the top of the mountain with him and talking with my family in ways we've never talked before..."

She went on like this, expressing all the wondrous changes that had happened in her life. "Now I'm really feeling pleasurable sensations," she reported.

"So I'd like to teach you about *Toning*," I said. "Take a deep breath and let out a long sound all the way to the end." When she had done this for a few breaths, I asked her to pretend the sound was the song of all the pleasures in her life. She sang the tone for quite some time and eventually reported that she could feel pleasurable tingling in her feet.

I then told her about Laurel Keyes [9] who had developed Toning and had taught it to Rolfers [7] at the Rolf Institute in Boulder. She had worked in hospitals with dying people and found that if the person could say the word, "Thrust", they would recover. The idea was that to say that word, they would have to send energy out with the TH sound, thus starting to breathe more deeply and create more energy in the body. Remember, sound *is* energy. I refer you to my chapter "Sound as Energy" for more on Laurel Keyes [9].

Sometimes I have a student *Tone* when they feel sad. After they get into making the sound with long, long exhalations, I ask them to pretend the sound is all the things they want to say to the person or I ask them to sing the story of their grief with the tone,"Ohhhh". If they continue, they will often come into their tears, sometimes sobbing or even wailing, which we do not often get a chance to do in this culture. *Toning* can be used in healing yourself or others, if you hold them in your thoughts or intentions. You can also heal from a distance, again, holding them in your intentions.

I then told her how, in the late '70s, when I was doing a two week workshop in Berkeley, my 17 year old daughter who was working in Colorado, had had a traumatic experience the day before. I asked the group to Tone her name, which we did for about 20 minutes. My daughter later reported to me that she had (after 24 hours of anxiety) finally relaxed, felt peaceful and fell asleep at the exact time we had been toning. I now asked my student if she would like to tone someone's name.

"Oh, my husband. He has been so hassled at work." So we toned his name for 10 minutes. She then left, feeling so much calmer than when she had arrived.

Later, she called me, reporting that she had checked in with her husband and he said his whole day had turned around at that time. If you have a hard time believing this, I'd remind you that energetically, all things, animate and inanimate, including thought is all connected. Here is a story that may help.

One day a grandfather took his five year old granddaughter up the mountain. After some time they sat on the grass and he said, "Watch that meadow over there."

"Ohh!" the little girl exclaimed. "It's a Unicorn!" She paused. "But Unicorns don't exist."

"That's what everyone says," said the grandfather, "and so it is very hard 'to see' a Unicorn. And it's even harder to 'believe' you are seeing a Unicorn. But the hardest thing of all, is to 'remember', that you 'believed', you saw a Unicorn."

From Crawly Feeling to Pleasure

Sofia comes forward with her pillow and lies down with it on her stomach. She says her stomach is always agitated, with a crawly feeling which has been with her all her life. Her mother told her that when they brought her home from the hospital, she cried and cried until they put her on her stomach and she has slept on her stomach ever since.

Bioenergetics [2] teaches that stomach difficulties are a sign of fear and because she is telling me she came home from the hospital with this, I imagine she has had this even in the womb. I do not say this to her though and just ask her if she is willing to let herself drift back to when this first was with her. She agrees and is quiet, breathing. I wait for her response.

Soon she begins to clutch her pillow and rock her body, mumbling something. Then louder, she says "No, no, no. I don't want to leave. It's crazy out there. I can hear them. Noooo!" She starts to cry. It sounds very young.

When this happens, I sit very still, holding the space and just witnessing for the person. This is a way of acknowledging their truth, something we are always wanting. When we interrupt someone's emotions, we deny their experience and their inner truth. I notice that she has really learned how to cry. So many people have shut this ability off and cannot let themselves have this experience. Since she has worked with me a while, she has learned to use her sound and to take that crying sound all the way to the end of the breath. This allows the body to release all the tension held around that particular trauma. Babies do this naturally unless they are stopped and taught to repress it. Most people have, so I often have to teach the student how to wail (expel all the breath with sound).

Finally, Sofia is quiet again. I ask her how she is feeling now in her stomach. She replies that the wormy feeling is going away. I tell her to just breathe and watch the letting go. Soon she reports a pleasurable pulse low in her abdomen.

She lies there quietly for a time and then people give her feedback (basically what that brought up for them or how she appears now — that her face looks softer or younger which is often the case, or that her breathing looks deeper).

It is important to note that even though this was a preverbal experience, some people put words to it. Others cannot, perhaps only having an experience. Some know it is preverbal, others are confused, wondering if it was real.

This was my experience with a piece of my own work when I experienced biting my mother's breast and was so puzzled by this that I questioned my mother. You can read more about this in the chapter on My Exploration Into Light.

The Best of all Worlds

Sandra had known him for a long time. They were really great friends and had decided to make it a more intimate relationship. "As soon as I'm in a relationship, I find things wrong with it." she said. "Now I feel like I'm in a box." I asked her to say that a few more times and feel her body. As she did this she began putting her hands over her eyes. I asked her to keep them there and say "I don't want to see it.".

Soon she was crying and telling about how her mother would never let her cry or have other emotions. She screamed and then she went numb again. She said she didn't feel anything. Then she put her hands over her eyes again and I asked her what she didn't want to see in the relationship. "He needs a lot more space than I do. He likes to be alone a lot. He doesn't want to talk about feelings .....I have to be numb."

"Make yourself numb...even number. And say, I'm numbing out. I'm numbing out," I told her. She said this over and over. Then I asked her what she was feeling. "More

108

relaxed, pleasure," was the reply. This demonstrates that when I let myself experience myself as I am without judgement, and verbalize it, I change. This is a simple definition of Self Acceptance Training.

I had a sense that there was more to the story and that she was still holding back so I asked her to come to the wall and sit with her back to it and push back against the wall as hard as she could. As she was doing this I suddenly had the words come to me, "I have the best of all worlds." I asked her to say them and immediately her throat got tight. When there is *any* change in the body it is a sign to me that there is truth to the words. (In this case, a numb throat which suddenly gets some energy flowing will be experienced as tight. Similarly, just as a hand that has been held tight will be experienced as pain and then become numb, will feel pain first when you start to open it). I reminded her of that and had her say, "I have the best of all worlds," a few more times. Suddenly she reported that her throat had opened and was feeling very pleasurable. She said it had not felt that open in years.

"It's true, I do have the best of all worlds. He is wonderful when I'm with him and I have friends that let me have my emotions and I have my profession which I love and I have my sons. I do have the best of all worlds. I was just trying to have it all with him --- and putting myself in the box to do it".

Everyone commented on how soft and relaxed she looked. Indeed, she was glowing. This was a wonderful lesson that came from her after she had discharged the fear and pain. It is true that we cannot get everything we need from one person and many relationships fail from trying. Also, she is more extroverted than he and extroverts get their energy renewed by being with others while introverts get their energy renewed by being alone [17].

Thinking vs. Feeling

The Musk Deer

"I was thinking last night, about how people saw me and then I wondered who I really was. It's like I have been searching for myself all my life. Who am I really? I've searched for myself in people, in communities, in activities. But I still don't know."

It was obvious to me that Frank was talking about the capital 'S' - Self (that aspect of ourselves that is merged in Divinity or what some call God). I knew that Frank was a seeker, had been a priest and is an avid meditator.

I asked him to reach his arms out, open his heart and call out, 'Where are you?'. He did this several times and his body started to shake. This is a common reaction when energy starts to move and is very pleasurable if allowed. He also started to cry, "I long for you." over and over. I asked him to allow himself to feel this longing, to realize that the *longing* is also the *love* for the Divine. The heart holds both – the love and the longing. He continued reaching, and calling, tears rolling down his cheeks.

After some time he became very calm. "I feel peace." Then he told us that he had bought the DVD of *The Little Prince* for two little neighbor girls and he just realized that he was the Little Prince, forgetting to trust his heart.

"We are all like that Frank," I said. "Each one of us. We are all seekers, searching for that Oneness. Some people try to find it in other people, their lovers, their children, or some try to find it in material possessions, career building or sometimes in drugs. We are all seeking it."

"We are like the Musk Deer," I said.

"What is that?" he asked.

"The Musk Deer," I explained, "is dropped from the mother's womb and smells this incredible smell. He struggles to his feet and begins to run after the smell. He runs and runs, searching, searching, searching, until he finally drops in exhaustion. Panting, he again smells it but is too tired to get up. Suddenly, he realizes that the incredible smell is coming from within him."

We are all like the Musk Deer, searching outside ourselves for what can only be found inside, that connection to the Divine.

I Can Deal With It

Beverly had been coming to my Wednesday afternoon women's group for quite a while and often worked on one relationship after another which would leave her devastated and feeling a lot of low self esteem. Finally seeing her pattern of choosing men who always had someone on the side, she took a six months hiatus from dating to work on getting strong within herself.

This particular day she came in very happy and announced she was in a new relationship, had met him in an art program and he was incredible. Not only was he everything she wanted but he also was into self growth. And yes, he was honest enough to tell her he had another girlfriend but, "Now I'm strong enough to handle that!" she told us.

She looked at me and said, "I am a lot stronger than before, I've grown a lot, I'm not so needy and I really know I can deal with this now. And that's what I want to work on."

I said, "Okay, come into the center, breathe into your body, and tell me what you are aware of."

Sitting cross legged in the center of the circle, she looked very happy. "I feel a lot of excitement. I'm very excited to tell you all about him."

"So tell *him* this, how you are excited to share him with the group and how you can handle the situation now." I wanted to have her make this an I-Thou experience by talking 'to' him rather than 'about' him, thus bringing up more truth from the body.

"Well, Jake, I'm really excited to tell everyone about you. I have worked really hard for six months and I feel ready to have this relationship. I know you have another girlfriend but I can.....augh, augh." She started dry heaving and this lasted for about 30 seconds.

When she stopped she look at me with a sly grin. "I guess my body knows more than my head."

I often relate this piece of work to students because it graphically shows how easily we can fool ourselves with our thinking and rob the body of it's truth.

The Many Faceted Jewel

Brenda first came to me at thirty, angry at both parents, saying her father had sexually abused her for years and her mother wouldn't believe her. She wanted me to help her to disown them, to get them out of her head and out of her life. I told her I would prefer to help her work through all the sadness, anger, loss and betrayal and see where that left her in relationship to them.

So for several years we worked with all that material. Finally, she was able to write a letter to her parents, telling them she loved them and forgave them. When her father was diagnosed with cancer a few years later, she felt healed enough to hold him in his last hours and tell him she loved him.

Occasionally the old pain would resurface and we would work on it again.

For many people this is a lifelong journey. The damage can be very deep. When she enrolled in a one day group, she didn't know what she would explore as her life was pretty peaceful. She started by breathing and noticing her body sensations.

Soon she was crying. I asked her what was happening.

She replied that she was back at the first time he touched her. The family is watching TV and he's asked her to sit on his lap. Reminding her to stay in her body, that it is okay to feel this, I asked her to talk to him, to verbalize how she feels.

"Why are you doing this Dad? I don't like it." She started to sob, "I hate you! I hate you!"

I asked her why she was calling him Dad. "If you are only five years old, wouldn't you call him Daddy?"

"I would NEVER call him Daddy!!" she yelled, vehemently. "After what he did to me?!"

I then realized that the next step in her healing was to reconnect with her trusting little girl. This was not about her father and somehow condoning his actions, but about her sense of wholeness. To be whole, we must identify with each facet of the incredible many faceted jewel of our being. She had lost her trusting, little girl and needed to re-experience this part of herself.

I then asked her if she was willing to do a re-taping of the event. Because she had worked with me for so long and had seen the results of this tool before with others in groups she had been in, she agreed to do it.

In the re-taping fantasy, I asked her to go into her body, to go back to the scene *and THIS TIME* he holds her on his lap and they are watching the TV together. I left her in that space for a time.

After a period of silence, she began to sob. I asked her what was happening. "He DOES love me! He DOES!!" She had gone back to a time before the incidents began. Her face softened in a pink glow.

Incest as well as rape, BOTH BEING ABUSE, take a long time to work through. There are so many repressed emotions involved that the often confused child or adult can not express and each of these need to be explored and experienced, perhaps many times. However, with each experience of revisiting, allowing and feeling the repressed emotion, the adult comes away with a stronger sense of self. When I *feel* and *express* my emotions and sensations without acting them out on others, I validate who I am. Sometimes people who have been abused and have not worked it through can consciously or unconsciously repeat the pattern. That is why it is imperative to bring this to awareness, because it can alleviate the victimization of others.

Testimonial

I started my career working with teenagers and found that children and young people are very open to exploring themselves and their potential. I have been so honored to have witnessed changes in so many lives. I could tell you about working with my five year old granddaughter who was so frightened by the movie, "Beauty and the Beast". Using a doll with two heads, (one the handsome prince and the other, the beast), and Gestalt techniques, I had her talk to the beast and the beast (me), talk back until she was no longer frightened. I could also tell you about a seven year old boy who fought a violent battle between two of his plastic super hero toys. One represented himself and the other his father whom he was furious with but was helpless to express it. Or I could tell you of the psychiatrist who wrote about how he used SAT on himself during a heart attack. The list goes on, the many lives that have benefitted from this work.

The following is one of my favorite testimonials, the most endearing to me because of my intense interest in the education of our young, underprivileged, and/or underachieving children. I believe that many learning disabilities are formed by traumatic experiences in the child's life.

A positive outlet for children's anger?

Here is a testimonial from a teacher who has been in my Professional Training Group for a number of years. After some foot stomping visualization and relaxation activities, these

5th grade ISAT tutoring students, transformed their anger into positive energy, creating this collage of positive thoughts.

"Many students in my school district have hectic, sometimes violent home lives. This affects their abilities to learn at school, although most of these students are smart enough to succeed. I work with a group of 5th grade students who are not achieving at their grade level on the state testing.

As an experiment, I have implemented some visualization techniques during my class time with them. I have them lay on the ground with their knees bent and their feet flat on the floor. They stomp their feet and slap their hands and say "No!" They can say "No" to homework, "No" to ISAT tutoring, "No" to babysitting, "No" to washing dishes, whatever it is in their lives that they don't like. Or they can simply say, "No".

After this exercise they relax and close their eyes, and I walk them through a visualization of floating on a cloud. Next, they imagine running through a field in the warm sun. They are free, no homework, no washing dishes, etc. Then they go in the house and get a healthy drink and turn on the TV. On the TV they see themselves doing whatever activities they are interested in. They are excelling, they are catching passes, making touchdowns, and scoring goals in soccer, hitting homers, singing and dancing on stage, whatever their dreams are. Then, they switch the channel and they are watching themselves at school. They are reading and understanding what they read. They know the answers. They see the teacher returning their tests with A's and B's. They are behaving and following all the rules. They are imagining the principal giving them the certificate for the honor roll.

After a few weeks, one of my students came in and said, "Ms. Edwards, we need to do that visualizing thing, cuz I am SO MAD!" Some other students chimed in and began arguing with each other. As soon as they began yelling and blaming each other, I interrupted them and said we could discuss it after the visualization. They were so mad that they wanted to stand up and stomp their feet. They were even swinging imaginary bats. This went on quite a bit longer than usual. When they were done they laid down to do the visualizing. As I came to the end of the cloud visualization, one student asked if they could stay in the cloud a little longer. Of course, we did. When the visualization was complete, I waited for them to get up. We had planned on doing a computer program that the kids had been very eager to play, so I imagined that they would jump up and run upstairs. No one moved. Nervously, I said, "OK, you can visualize a little longer if you'd like." (Authors note: This is Self Acceptance Training, to allow whatever is, with awareness and wait for change.) The students started to come to life.

Just as we were getting ready to go upstairs, one student asked if she could write something on the board. I said, "Sure as long as it's positive". She proceeded to write, "Be Happy!" in huge letters on the board. All the other students wanted to contribute as well. They created this beautiful collage of positive sayings. What ever had incited such anger was never mentioned and many of them ended up scoring 'meets standards' and 'exceeds standards' on the portion of the testing they were working on for that day. What an extremely exciting day this was for me to see what incredible tools these are. In allowing these students to feel their anger and release it, it was literally transformed into positive creative energy."

Here is a photo of their collage.

Aimee Edwards

Elementary school teacher

Bibliography

1. Author, Robert Scaer, M.D. Uploaded by Cherie McCoy. (2016, June 25). How the Brain Works in Trauma [Video file]. Viewable at https://youtu.be/BYKRR9Bvm_M

2. Dr. Alexander Lowen, *Bioenergetics: The Revolutionary Therapy That Uses the Language of the Body to Heal the Problems of the Mind*. ISBN-13: 978-0140194715

3. David Perlmutter, *Grain Brain: The Surprising Truth about Wheat, Carbs, and Sugar--Your Brain's Silent Killers*. ISBN-13: 978-0316234801

4. Alan Watts, *The Wisdom of Insecurity: A Message for an Age of Anxiety*. ISBN-13: 978-0307741202

5. Tom Biesanz. (2016, June 25). Transcripts of lectures by Dick Olney on ALIVE and REAL. Retrieved from http://www.aliveandreal.com/

6. Roslyn Moore, *Walking in Beauty: A Collection of Psychological Insights and Spiritual Wisdom of Dick Olney*. ISBN-13: 978-0964699908

7. Ida Rolf, *Rolfing: The Integration of Human Structures*, ISBN-13: 978-0064650960

8. Inst. of Psychology, *Magazine of Neural Science at the U. Of Glasgow*. 4 Emotions

9. Laurel Elizabeth Keyes, *Toning: The Creative Power of the Voice*. ISBN-13: 978-0875161761

10. Wayne Dyer, *The Power of Intention*. ISBN-13: 978-1401902162

11. David R. Hawkins M.D. Ph.D., *Power vs. Force. The Eye of the I.* ISBN-13: 978-1401945077

12. Wilhelm Reich, *Character Analysis.* ISBN-13: 978-0374509804

13. Dr. Fritz Perls. *In And Out The Garbage Pail.* ISBN-13: 978-0939266173

14. Dr. Grantly Dick-Read, *Childbirth Without Fear: The Principles and Practice of Natural Childbirth.* ISBN-13: 978-1780660554

15. Desmond Tutu, *The Book of Forgiving: The Fourfold Path for Healing Ourselves and Our World.* ISBN-13: 978-0062203571

16. Minghui.org. (July 2, 2016) Traditional Chinese Culture as Reflected through the Concept of "Male Left, Female Right" [Webpage]. Viewable at http://www.clearwisdom.net/html/articles/2010/3/24/115543.html

17. Kelly McGonigal, *The Willpower Instinct: How Self-Control Works, Why It Matters, and What You Can Do to Get More of It.* ISBN-13: 978-1583335086

18. Wikipedia. (2016, June 25). *Eye movement desensitization and reprocessing [Webpage].* Viewable at https://en.wikipedia.org/wiki/Eye_movement_desensitization_and_reprocessing

19. Friedrich Salomon Perls, Uploaded by paulchabe. (2016, June 25). *Fritz Perls Clip2* [Video file]. Viewable at https://youtu.be/AlayqPwDuz0

20. Wikipedia. (2016, June 25). Ohr [Webpage]. Viewable at https://en.wikipedia.org/wiki/Ohr

21. World Peace Project. (2016, June 26). *Washington crime study shows 23.3% drop in violent crime due to*

meditating group [Webpage]. Viewable at http://www.worldpeacegroup.org/washington_crime_study.html

22. Rhonda Byrne, *The Secret.* ISBN-13: 978-1582701707

Learn more about
Self Acceptance Training at

http://www.selfacceptance.us/

Made in the USA
San Bernardino, CA
22 August 2016